The Bette Midler Scrapbook

The Bette Midler Scrapbook

Allison J. Waldman

A Citadel Press Book
Published by Carol Publishing Group

Copyright © 1997 Allison J. Waldman

A Citadel Press Book
Published by Carol Publishing Group
Citadel Press is a registered trademark of Carol Communications,Inc.

Editorial, sales and distribution, and rights and permissions inquiries should be addressed to Carol Publishing Group, 120 Enterprise Avenue, Secaucus, N.J. 07094.

In Canada: Canadian Manda Group, One Atlantic Avenue, Suite 105, Toronto, Ontario M6K 3E7

Carol Publishing Group books may be purchased in bulk at special discounts for sales promotion, fund-raising, or educational purposes. Special editions can be created to specifications. For details, contact Special Sales Department, Carol Publishing Group, 120 Enterprise Avenue, Secaucus, N.J. 07094.

Designed by Andrew B. Gardner

Manufactured in the United States of America

10 9 8 7 6 5 4 3 2 1

Library of Congress Cataloging-in-Publication Data

Waldman, Allison J.
    The Bette Midler scrapbook / Allison J. Waldman.
        p.   cm.
    "A Citadel Press book."
    ISBN 0-8065-1848-0 (pb)
    1. Midler, Bette.   2. Midler, Bette—Miscellanea.   I. Title.
ML420.M43W35   1997
782.42164'092—dc21
    [B]   97-19817
                                                                              CIP
                                                                              MN

This book is dedicated to the "wind beneath my wings"... my nieces and nephews, from A to Z: Amanda, Ben, Chelsea, Erik, Evan, Ian, Jillian, Jordyn, and Zachary.

Contents

(Above) *Bette Midler's prints in cement at the MGM Park in Disneyworld (Walter McBride/Retna Ltd.)* (Opposite) *Long before Madonna, Bette did concerts in her underwear.*

ONE

Just the Facts

Name: Bette Midler

Nickname(s): The Librarian; "Harriet Craig" (i.e., the title character in *Craig's Wife*, a play by George Kelly, made into several movies, about a wife who's a compulsive cleaner)

Alter Egos: The Divine Miss M; Soph; Baby Divine; Delores DeLago

Occupation: Singer/Actress/Writer/Producer

Height: 5'1"

Weight: 115 lbs.

Hair: Currently champagne blond; originally foxy brown; occasionally fire-engine red

Eyes: Brown

Bra Size: 34 DD

Date of Birth: December 1, 1945

Birthplace: Honolulu, Hawaii

Mother: Ruth Schindel

Father: Fred "Chesty" Midler

Siblings: Susan, Daniel, Judith (deceased)

Religion: Judaism

Educational Background: AIEA School of Hawaii; Radford High School, Class of 1963; University of Hawaii

Marital Status: Married Martin von Haselberg, December 16, 1985, in Las Vegas, Nevada

Children: Sophie Frederica Alohilani von Haselberg, born November 14, 1986

(Opposite)Bette has won a handful of American Comedy Awards.

Astrological Sign: "Sagittarius with Aries rising, a Scorpio moon, and lots of Leo—almost completely a fire chart."

Motto: "Fuck 'em if they can't take a joke!"

Happiness Is: "A plate of linguine at Umberto's. White clam sauce, thank you, with lots of fat, juicy clams."

Favorite Pastimes: Reading, cleaning, cooking, gardening

Starts the Day With: Two double cappuccinos

Pet: Puddles, a Jack Russell terrier

Her Wish for Her Child: "Good health, a great education, a good head start, and a lot of laughs."

Political Affiliation: Democrat

Charities: The Manhattan Restoration Project, Adopt-a-Highway, AIDS Project Los Angeles, Get Out the Vote

Major Awards: Two Emmys; four Grammys; a special Tony; four Golden Globes; APLA Commitment to Life; American Cinemathèque; American Comedy Awards; Hasty Pudding Theatrical Club's Woman of the Year; multiple gold and platinum albums and singles

First Job: Working at a pineapple factory in Hawaii

If She Were a Boat: "I'd be a tugboat. Squat, hardworking, homey, with a touch of whimsy. I've always thought of myself as a Tugboat Annie type."

Theater Credits: *Miss Nefertiti Regrets* (Cafe LaMama); *Cinderella Revisited* (13th Street Theater); *Fiddler on the Roof* (Majestic Theater); *Salvation* (off-Broadway)

Film Credits: *Hawaii* (extra) (1966); *The Thorn* (a.k.a. *The Divine Mr. J*) (1971); *The Rose* (1979); *Divine Madness* (1980); *Jinxed* (1982);

(Greg Gorman/Atlantic Records)

Down and Out in Beverly Hills (1986); *Ruthless People* (1986); *Outrageous Fortune* (1987); *Oliver & Company* (animated) (1988); *Big Business* (1988); *Beaches* (1989); *Stella* (1990); *Scenes From a Mall* (1991); *For the Boys* (1991); *Hocus Pocus* (1993); *Gypsy* (TVM) (1993); *Get Shorty* (cameo) (1995); *The First Wives Club* (1996); *That Old Feeling* (1997)

Recording Credits: *The Divine Miss M* (1972); *Bette Midler* (1973); *Songs for the New Depression* (1976); *Live at Last* (1977); *Broken Blossom* (1977); *Thighs and Whispers* (1979); *The Rose* (1980); *Divine Madness* (1980); *No Frills* (1983); *Mud Will Be Flung Tonight!* (1985); *Oliver & Company* (1988); *Beaches* (1988); *Some People's Lives* (1990); *For the Boys* (1991); *Experience the Divine: Bette Midler's Greatest Hits* (1993); *Gypsy* (1993); *Bette of Roses* (1995); *The Hunchback of Notre Dame* (1996)

Concert Credits: *Continental Baths* (1970–72); *Carnegie Hall* (1972); *Philharmonic Hall at Lincoln Center* (1972); *the Divine Miss M Tour* (1973); *Bette at the Palace* (1973); *Clams on the Half-Shell Revue* (1975); *the Depression Tour* (1975); *the Club Tour* (1977); *the world tour* (1978); *Bette Midler: Divine Madness!* (1979); *De Tour* (1982); *Experience the Divine* (1993–94); *Diva Las Vegas* (1996–97)

Most Successful Album: *Beaches* (triple platinum)
Most Successful Single: "Wind Beneath My Wings"
Most Successful Film (at box office): *The First Wives Club*

Bette with the love of her life, her daughter, Sophie (Bill Davila/Retna Ltd.)

Posing with her star on
Hollywood Boulevard
(UPI/Corbis-Bettman)

Two

In My Life:
The Bette Midler
Chronology

December 1, 1945

Bette Midler is born in Honolulu, Hawaii, the third child of Fred "Chesty" Midler and his wife Ruth Schindel Midler.

September 1950

Bette Midler starts elementary school at AIEA School of Hawaii.

1955

Fifth grader Bette discovers that she has a way with comedy. With classmate Barbara Nagy, she does comic sketches for their friends. When Bette can't remember the words, she improvises, coming up with even funnier material. "It was so strange. People were laughing at something I did. It was a real nice feeling."

1956

Bette enters a school talent contest and wins the first prize—$2—by singing "Lullaby of Broadway."

December 1, 1958

Ruth Midler finally allows a mature, thirteen-year-old Bette to get a brassiere. "I used to get teased and I remember coming home weeping, so she broke down and got me one for my birthday. Oh, I was so relieved!"

1959

Bette enters Radford High School, where she excels in academics. With two girlfriends, she forms a folksinging group called the Pieridine Three. They perform at school functions.

1961

Thanks to her good grades, Bette is accepted into the Regents Club, an academic honor society for girls, and soon becomes the club president. Bette, who had been considered rather quiet and an egghead despite her singing and performing, changes her image to become more popular. She becomes a class clown. According to classmate Penny Sellers, "She seemed less studious. Her raucous laugh made us all giggle, and her witty remarks were—well—bawdy."

1962

The change in personality results in Bette winning friends and influencing people. "I came into glory in high school. I was even popular," Bette recalled. "It was a real surprise. . . . In high school I became a person. That was when I began to realize I wasn't as bad as I thought." Bette meets Beth Ellen Childers, and they quickly become best friends. "She was the funniest person I ever met. . . . She made me believe in myself. She made me feel okay to be who I was. My family never made me feel this way. She drew me out of myself."

1963

In her senior year at Radford, Bette is voted class president and "most talkative." She grabs the lead in the senior class play, *Our Hearts Were Young and Gay.* She also is a member of the Speech Club and wins the statewide championship for dramatic interpretation.

1964

After graduation, Bette's theatrical ambitions are doused by a dose of reality. She gets a job on the assembly line at a pineapple factory. Bette remembers, "All day long I'd sit there and pick out the pineapple slices. . . . It was really sickening, but I needed money." She moves out

Hawaiian Jewish Princess
(from 1976 concert program)

of her family home and enters the University of Hawaii to study theater. She appears in *The Typists*.

1965

Beth Ellen Childers, Bette's best friend from high school, dies in an auto accident. Bette is devastated. "She was the only real friend I ever had. My mom and I were close, but when Beth Ellen died, I carried on so much my mom thought we must have been lesbians."

April 1965

After a role in *The Cherry Orchard* at the University of Hawaii, Bette answers a call for extra work on the film version of James Michener's bestseller *Hawaii*. Ten local actors are chosen, including Bette, who is cast as the seasick wife of a missionary.

November 1965

To shoot additional scenes for *Hawaii*, the company moves to a soundstage in Hollywood. It's Bette's chance to get to the mainland, and she takes it. She has already decided to save her money from the movie to relocate to New York City. "I thought that if I had to have a career in the theater, the way to do it was to get a job on the New York stage. I mean, they don't have much theater in Chicago or Cleveland. See, I figured it was the only place to go."

December 1965

Hawaii wraps in Hollywood, and Bette heads east to Manhattan. She moves into the Broadway Central Hotel, renting a room for $15 a week.

1966

Bette struggles to get work on the stage. She enrolls in the Herbert Berghof Studio to study acting and also takes dancing and singing

In **Cinderella Revisited***, 1966
(from 1976 concert program)*

lessons. She picks up odd jobs to pay the rent, including selling gloves at Stern's department store, typing at Columbia University, checking hats at a New York restaurant, and even go-go dancing at a club in Union City, New Jersey.

Spring 1966
Bette auditions for *Miss Nefertiti Regrets,* a satirical comedy by Tom Eyen, to be staged at Cafe LaMama. She sings Kurt Weill's "Pirate Jenny" and impresses Eyen, who casts her in the play. The short run is revived a few months later, this time with Bette in the lead role of Nefertiti.

Summer 1966
Bette heads to the Borscht Belt, New York's Catskill Mountains. The plethora of summer hotels is packed with tourists waiting to be entertained, and Bette finds work in a variety of showcases. She is also part of *An Evening of Tradition,* performing pieces from the works of Jewish writers Sholom Aleichem and Paddy Chayevsky. It is a preview of sorts for Bette—she will soon become one of Tevye's daughters in *Fiddler on the Roof,* the Tony Award–winning musical based on Sholom Aleichem's stories.

Fall 1966
Bette is cast in Tom Eyen's schizophrenic comedy *Cinderella Revisited.* For children, the piece is done following the fairy tale tradition. For adults, the title is changed to *Sinderella,* and a racier version enacted. Also at this time, Bette auditions for *Fiddler on the Roof.* She is turned down initially because the casting director considers her "too Jewish." Later on, she tries again and is deemed "not Jewish enough." Finally, she lands a spot in the chorus; she also understudies the role of Tzeitel.

1967
After being let go from the *Fiddler* chorus, Bette learns that the role of Tzeitel is being recast. She applies, and in an odd twist indicative of backstage politics, the casting director offers Bette her old spot in the chorus if she gives up her audition for the Tzeitel role. Bette is anxious to be seen by *Fiddler* director and Broadway legend Jerome Robbins. "I wanted to get a look at [him]. I worship the ground he dances upon, so I said, 'I'm sorry, I'm taking the audition.' " Bette correctly surmises that the casting director has someone else in mind and fears Bette will snatch the role. Eschewing the chorus part, Bette takes a risk and does

the audition. Fortunately for her, Robbins chooses her for Tzeitel. With a regular, healthier paycheck, Bette moves to an apartment on West 75th Street.

1968

Bette's older sister, Judith, comes to New York. She plans to stay with Bette and study filmmaking. One night while going to meet Bette at the theater, Judy is killed in a freak traffic accident. Bette is contacted by police and has to identify her sister's corpse. She then has to call the family in Hawaii and break the awful news. As Fred Midler later reveals, "An auto came out of one of those indoor garages and smashed her right up against the wall. Mutilated her complete-ly. The funeral directors wouldn't even permit us to view the body." Although Bette is strong and emotionally together during the shiva (the Jewish period of mourning), the trauma of losing her sister stays with her always. When Bette's first album is released, it is dedicated to Judith.

Fall 1968

Bette begins spreading her wings by singing at local New York cabarets, like Hilly's and the Improvisation. She experiments with song styles, doing material as varied as "God Bless the Child" and "Lullaby of Broadway." Gradually, Bette becomes more enamored of her club work than the repetitious grind of *Fiddler*. During this period, Bette and Ben Gillespie—a *Fiddler* dancer—form a great friendship. He teaches her about music, art, costume, and the world. According to Bette, "He was my mentor. He opened up the world for me . . . taught me about music and dance and drama and poetry and light and color and sound and movement. He taught me grandeur. He inspired me not to be afraid and to understand what the past had to offer me."

1969

Bud Friedman, owner of the Improvisation, becomes Bette's first man-ager. She begins singing nightly at the Improv, testing new material

In **Fiddler on the Roof,** *1967–69 (from 1976 concert program)*

and shaping her act. Bette leaves *Fiddler* after nearly three years. When actress Marta Heflin, a friend from *Fiddler*, is cast in an off-Broadway show called *Salvation*, it leads to a chance for Bette. Bette wins Marta's role (a nymphomaniac who is saved at a revival meeting) in the New York production when her friend goes west to star in the L.A. edition of the show.

Spring 1970

Bob Ellston, a former acting teacher of Bette's from the Herbert Berghof Studio, recommends her cabaret act to Steve Ostrow. Ostrow, owner of a gay bathhouse called the Continental Baths, goes to see her at the Improv and offers her $50 a weekend—one show per night—to sing at his club. Despite the unusual circumstances, Bette agrees.

July 1970

Bette opens at the Continental Baths. Her first shows are heavy on music—mostly ballads and torch songs—and devoid of comedy. With the help of Bill Hennessy, another *Fiddler* friend, Bette begins adding more humor to her act. She quickly realizes that she can push the envelope of outrageousness with the gay crowd. They respond to her "divine" grandeur and campy humor in a positive way, giving Bette more and more confidence in her performing abilities. Word spreads in the gay community that she is a sensation. The Continental Baths is soon filled to capacity for Bette's shows. Bette acquires a new pianist at this time, a skinny young songwriter named Barry Manilow.

July–August 1970

As her shows at the Continental Baths progress, Bette's affinity for the word "divine" becomes her trademark. She begins to be introduced as the Divine Miss M. Bud Friedman gets Bette booked on *The Tonight Show* with Johnny Carson. Initially, she is invited just to sing, but on her second *Tonight Show*, she makes it to the couch and converses with Carson. The two hit it off, forming a friendship that will last more than twenty-five years. Thanks to Carson, Bette Midler begins to become known nationally.

September 1970

Bette appears at Mr. Kelly's in Chicago, opening for comic Jackie Vernon. She tones down her more bawdy, colorful, "gay-oriented" humor, but still manages to make a big impression.

(Gary Gershoff/Retna Ltd.)

Winter 1971

Bette does a small but integral role in a low-budget picture about Jesus Christ. She's paid $250 to play the Virgin Mary in *The Greatest Story Ever Overtold* (later retitled *The Divine Mr. J*).

Spring 1971

Bette stars in the Seattle Opera Company's production of the Who's rock opera *Tommy*, playing both Mrs. Walker and the Acid Queen. She stops the show as the Acid Queen, singing her heart out and appearing on stage in a g-string and ruby-studded bra.

Summer 1971

Bette returns to Mr. Kelly's, this time opening for Mort Sahl. She meets a young musician named Michael Federal, and they begin seeing each other. When Bette returns to New York, Michael goes with her. Aside from being her lover, Michael becomes the bass player in a band that Bette forms to back her up.

September 1971

Bette returns to the Continental Baths, this time backed by her own newly formed band—including Michael Federal on bass and Barry Manilow on piano. Because of Bette's rising star, Ostrow opens the Baths to both men and women. Many movers and shakers—including Andy Warhol and Mick Jagger—venture uptown to see Bette's act. Bette's show is recorded on black-and-white video and years later resurfaces, including a clip in the *Art or Bust!* home video.

September 20, 1971

Bette opens at her first legitimate New York nightclub, Downstairs at the Upstairs, in the midst of hellacious weather and on the first night of the Jewish New Year, Rosh Hashanah. The crowds are sparse the first two nights. Bette places an ad in *Screw* magazine, tipping off her Continental Baths fans to her appearance at the Downstairs. Her ploy works, and soon the club is turning away customers. Her two-week gig is extended to over two months. John Wilson of the *New York Times* reviews her act, writing: "She has presence, she has a fine voice, she

Bette's tour included stops in the D.C. area. (Michael Gillespie Collection)

has wit and she has total mobility, including an unusually expressive face." On the negative side, Wilson complains about her humor, finding her satirical turns "unfocused," and the *Times* misspells her name in the headline, calling her "Milder."

October 1971
While at the Downstairs, Bette begins attracting recording company interest. Clive Davis, then in charge of Columbia Records, catches her act, but walks away without making an offer. On the other hand, Atlantic Records president Ahmet Ertegun likes Bette immediately.

Bette and Elton John were both guests on Cher's show. (CBS)

"She was overwhelming!" he later tells *Newsweek*. He offers her a deal with Atlantic, and Bette takes it.

Winter 1971–72

Bette continues playing clubs and universities around the country, backed by her band. She expands her repertoire, employing Barry Manilow's considerable talents as a musical director. She also adds a backup trio, the predecessors of the Harlettes. They are known at the time as MGM, short for Melissa Manchester, Gail Kantor, and Merle Miller.

February 1972

Bette appears at the Continental Baths for her "farewell" performance. She also begins working on her first Atlantic album, with Joel Dorn producing. Despite Bette's strong collaboration with Barry Manilow, Dorn eschews most of Manilow's arrangements. To capitalize on her club success, Bette makes a bold move. She has her agency book her a date at New York's premiere musical showcase, Carnegie Hall.

April 1972

Bette opens for Johnny Carson at the Sahara Hotel in Las Vegas. Although she is nervous about playing Vegas, she puts on a terrific show. *Variety*'s review compares her favorably with Barbra Streisand, Janis Joplin, and Mae West, concluding, "Miss Midler's obvious jitters on opening night will probably be dispelled early, leaving only the enormous chutzpah to come through naturally in her gabbity-gab and the unique quality of the voice and material to take precedence, as it should."

Spring 1972

Work on the album continues, but Bette tells Barry that it's no fun. While rehearsing for Carnegie Hall, Bette invites Barry to hear the final mix of the album. He is very disappointed, feeling the Dorn production fails to capture Bette's magic. "As I saw it, the Bette Midler album should be a milestone in records, not unlike Streisand's debut on records. This album wasn't. It was ordinary. Bette wasn't," Barry will recall in his memoir, *Sweet Life*.

May 1972

Bette plays a gig at the Bitter End in New York. She continues to pack in the crowds and gain more and more notoriety. *Newsweek* pays homage with a feature. "It all comes together to make her one of the freshest, most captivating of the new girl singers. Bette Midler is . . .

hot." Among those who come to see her at the Bitter End is Aaron Russo, a self-made promoter and show business wannabe.

June 23, 1972

Backed by a full orchestra, her girls, and Barry at the piano, and with New York at her feet, Bette is a huge hit at Carnegie Hall. Recalling the concert years later in his book, Manilow will write: "The show was spectacular. Bette was in her finest form. . . . She was saucy and haughty as usual, but the enormity of playing the hallowed Carnegie Hall was clearly having an effect. From within that confident, wisecracking character, she showed a genuine vulnerability I had never seen."

July 1972

Bette learns that Ertegun is disappointed with the work on her album. She confides in Manilow, and he lets her hear the bootleg tape he had made at Carnegie Hall. It cheers her up, but she is still down about the album. Barry plays the tape for Ertegun, selling him on the idea of bringing Manilow in to rework the arrangements and produce the sessions. Ertegun gives him the go-ahead.

August 1972

Bette performs in Central Park's Wollman Rink for the Schaefer Music Festival. People fill the rink and overflow into the park to hear and see Bette. She makes a concerted effort to present Bette Midler, not the Divine Miss M, and is overwhelmed by the audience's enthusiastic reaction. "That was really the happiest night of my life because I found out that they would take me for what I was, that I had succeeded and that I had achieved what I had started out to achieve, which was to come to myself, to come back to Bette Midler."

Fall 1972

Aaron Russo ingratiates himself into Bette's world, first as a friend and lover, but soon becomes her manager. He alienates many people in Bette's circle, but he proves himself to her. She leans heavily on him, allowing him to assume many of the business responsibilites she finds tedious and mundane.

November 1972

The Divine Miss M, Bette Midler's first album, is released by Atlantic Records to very favorable reviews. "Do You Want to Dance?" is released as a single.

November 1972

One last time, Bette does a "farewell" performance at the Continental Baths.

December 31, 1972

Bette welcomes the New Year—dressed in a 1973 banner and oversized diaper—on the stage of Philharmonic Hall at Lincoln Center. Her show is hailed in the *New York Times* with the headline "Good, Better, Best, Bette!"

February 1973

To promote her album and single, the *Divine Miss M Tour* begins a thirty-city odyssey in Rochester, New York. Aaron also books a summer tour. Bette calls Barry Manilow to conduct the band for her, but Barry is in the midst of promoting his own album. He convinces Aaron and Bette to give him a spot in the show—opening the second act—to do his own thing. In exchange, he agrees to conduct the band for Bette.

February 9, 1973

Bette does a guest turn on *Burt Bacharach—Opus Three,* his third TV special. She performs "Superstar" and "Boogie Woogie Bugle Boy."

April 23, 1973

Bette is given the *After Dark* Ruby Award as Performer of the Year.

June 1973

Bette makes a surprise appearance at the Gay Liberation Day parade in New York City.

July 1973

Barry Manilow and Bette work on her second album.

August 1973

Bette resumes touring, opening at the Merriwether Post Pavilion in Washington, D.C. Later in the month, she plays her hometown, Honolulu. Her mother, brother, and sister all come to see the show, but her father refuses the invitation.

September 1973

The tour moves to the Dorothy Chandler Pavilion in Los Angeles for a series of sold-out performances. While in L.A., Bette appears on *The Tonight Show* with Johnny Carson.

November 16, 1973

Bette Midler, Bette's second album, is released.

December 1973

The *Divine Miss M Tour* wraps up with an extended stay on Broadway at the Palace Theater. Bette's show is a huge success, setting a record with one-day sales of $148,000.

December 17, 1973

Bette appears on the cover of *Newsweek* magazine.

Winter 1974

Mike Nichols offers Midler the lead role in the Warren Beatty–Jack Nicholson farce *The Fortune*. Bette has a horrible meeting with Nichols at the Beverly Wilshire Hotel, showing up late and generally clashing with the award-winning director. The role ends up being played by Stockard Channing.

March 2, 1974

Bette wins the Grammy as Best New Artist. It is presented by Karen Carpenter, whom Bette had skewered in her concert act for her wholesome image and saccharine music.

April 1974

Johnny Carson presents a special Antoinette Perry Award—a Tony—to Bette. The special recognition is for her Palace Theater engagement, deemed "superior concert entertainment on the Broadway stage."

May 24, 1974

While Bette takes an extended vacation in Paris, *The Divine Mr. J*, the 1971 low-budget Canadian movie satirizing Christianity in which Bette appeared, is shown at the Festival Theater in New York. The ads promote the picture—originally titled *The Greatest Story Ever Overtold*—as Bette Midler's film debut. Aaron Russo manages to get the advertising to deemphasize Bette's participation and launches a publicity campaign to inform fans about the fact that Bette was not the star of the picture.

Bette was the highlight of the Grammys in 1975. (Brian Stein/Retna Ltd.)

Bette Midler IN CONCERT

Summer 1974

Bette keeps a low profile, refraining from performing. She spends more time in Paris, then returns to New York, where she reassesses her career options.

Winter 1974

Bette goes to Chicago to confer with Bruce Vilanch about ideas for her forthcoming Broadway concert. Based on his brilliant work creating Barbra Streisand's first two TV specials—*My Name Is Barbra* and *Color Me Barbra*— director Joe Layton is also enlisted by Midler.

February 1975

At the famed New York Oyster Bar in Grand Central Station, Bette announces her new Broadway concert, *The Clams on the Half-Shell Revue*. In addition to Bette, musician Lionel Hampton will also be part of the show.

February 16, 1975

Bette guests on Cher's TV special along with Elton John and Flip Wilson.

March 1, 1975

Bette goes to the Grammy Awards at the Uris Theater in New York City. She presents the Album of the Year Grammy to Stevie Wonder for *Fullfillingness' First Finale*. Her appearance receives major attention because she wears a 45rpm record in her hair like a hat. "It's 'Come Go With Me' by the Del-Vikings. It was a great record, but it's a better hat." Bette recalls winning the Best New Artist Grammy the year before, saying, "A year ago, Miss Karen Carpenter crowned me Best New Artist, and if that ain't the kiss of death, I don't know what is!"

April 14, 1975

Clams opens on Broadway to generally glowing reviews. The one-day sales of $200,000 is a record breaker. The previous record was also Bette's—$148,000 in 1973.

The Depression Tour—in Westchester, New York (Michael Gillespie Collection)

Spring 1975

In the midst of the Broadway run, Bette begins working on her next album, *Songs for the New Depression*.

May 18, 1975

Bette shocks the crowd for the United Jewish Appeal telethon by offering to drop her dress for Israel—for a big enough donation. When a pledge is made for $5,000, Bette unzips and struts on stage in a slip. In between her antics, Bette wows the audience by singing "Sentimental Journey," "Boogie Woogie Bugle Boy," "Hello in There," and "Friends."

November 16, 1975

Bette takes part in a tribute to Ira Gershwin at Avery Fisher Hall in New York, singing "They Can't Take That Away From Me."

Winter 1975

The *Clams* show is readied for touring. Renamed *the Depression Tour*—tying in to Bette's forthcoming album—the big production values of the Broadway show are scaled down.

December 2, 1975

While in California, rehearsing the show, Bette is stricken with appendicitis. She is rushed to the Beverly Hills Medical Center, where her appendix is removed. She returns to work a week later.

December 21, 1975

The Depression Tour opens in Berkeley, California.

December 31, 1975

The New Year's Eve show inspires Bette to the outrageous. She drops her dress and flashes the audience, crying "Happy New Year." Her behavior is applauded by the audience, but backstage, Aaron Russo is furious. He and Bette have a horrendous fight.

Febuary 1976

Songs for the New Depression, Bette's third album, is released.

February 6–7, 1976

Bette's *Depression Tour* show is taped at the Cleveland Music Hall. The two shows are later cut together to create the HBO special *The Fabulous Bette Midler.*

Ol' Red Hair Is Back *was a hit special for NBC. (Michael Gillespie Collection)*

February 15, 1976

In Buffalo, *the Depression Tour* has a setback. Seven members of the company are arrested when cocaine and marijuana are discovered in their Holiday Inn rooms.

February 17, 1976

Harvard presents Bette with the Hasty Pudding Theatrical Club's Woman of the Year award. She is feted in Cambridge, Massachusetts, including a parade in her honor.

June 19, 1976

Home Box Office airs *The Fabulous Bette Midler;* the uncensored TV concert is hailed by critics.

September 17, 1976

Bette guests on Neil Sedaka's TV special, doing "Drinking Again" and dueting with Sedaka on "Love Will Keep Us Together."

October 1976

Bette meets actor Peter Riegert, and they begin dating.

February 1977

Bette moves from New York to Los Angeles.

May 1977

Bette does a guest spot on Bing Crosby's TV special, singing with Crosby and the Mills Brothers.

June 1977

Live at Last, Bette's first double album and her first live concert on vinyl, is released to excellent reviews.

September 18, 1977

Aaron Russo and Bette produce a progay benefit at the Hollywood Bowl in Los Angeles. The "Night for Rights" includes Bette, Richard Pryor, Lily Tomlin, and others. Unfortunately, the event becomes infamous for Richard Pryor's out-of-control tirade against the audience.

Fall 1977

Rather than perform in large arenas with big productions, Bette decides to return to a more simple show in smaller nightclubs, launching a new tour—*the Club Tour.*

At a press conference about **The Rose,** *her first film* *(Michael Gillespie Collection)*

November 17, 1977

After nine months in the studio, *Broken Blossoms,* Bette's fifth album, is released.

December 7, 1977

Bette's first network TV special, *Ol' Red Hair Is Back,* premieres on NBC. Backed by the Harlettes and featuring actor Dustin Hoffman and clown Emmett Kelly, Bette reigns center stage. The production is topnotch. Produced by Gary Smith and directed by Dwight Hemion, who had earned Emmys for their work with Barbra Streisand and Frank Sinatra, among others, Bette's special shows off her diversity and innate talent. The show goes on to win the Emmy as the outstanding variety special of 1977.

January 1978

Bette's tour ends at the Copacabana in New York City.

April 24, 1978

Bette begins filming *The Rose,* her "official" film debut, a drama with music about the life of a self-destructive rock star.

July 18, 1978

The Rose wraps production. Bette immediately begins preparations for her first world concert tour.

Summer 1978

When the Harlettes announce that they do not want to do the tour, Bette puts an ad in the Hollywood trades for three new backup singer-dancers for the tour. Three are chosen from 250 applicants. They then embark upon an intense rehearsal schedule to prepare.

September 11, 1978

Bette's world tour commences in Seattle—her "out-of-town" tryout.

September 17, 1978

The world tour opens at the London Palladium. Although stunned by her audaciousness and cutting anti-British humor, the critics recognize

Bette went blond when she went Hollywood.

29

Bette was all smiles shooting The Rose.

Bette's brilliance. While Bette is overseas, her first TV special, *Ol' Red Hair Is Back*, is the Emmy winner for Outstanding Special—Variety or Music. She defeats, among others, her former musical director Barry Manilow, who was nominated for *The Second Barry Manilow Special*. Aaron Russo accepts the Emmy and forgets to thank Bette.

November 1978
The tour comes to a rousing finish in Sydney, Australia.

Winter 1979
Collecting her notes and journals, Bette begins writing a memoir of her world tour—*A View From a Broad,* for Simon and Schuster. Also, Bette ends her tumultuous relationship with personal manager Aaron Russo, firing him and assuming control of her career for the first time in years.

January 1979
Ruth Midler, Bette's beloved mother, dies. She'd suffered from leukemia and from breast and liver cancer.

Spring 1979
Bette works on tracks for her new album, *Thighs and Whispers*.

May 1979
Bette appears on *Saturday Night Live,* performing "Married Men" and "Martha."

August 24, 1979
Thighs and Whispers, Bette's latest studio album, is released.

Fall 1979
Bette and company prepare a U.S. version of the world tour, *Bette Midler: Divine Madness,* to play in select American cities before settling for a Broadway run at the Majestic Theater.

November 6, 1979
The Rose premieres in New York at the Ziegfeld Theater. Peter Riegert escorts Bette on the night of one of her greatest triumphs. The critics hail her performance, suggesting she'll win the Oscar.

December 5, 1979
Bette Midler: Divine Madness opens at the Majestic Theater in New York City for a six-week run.

Divine Madness *was Bette back on Broadway! (Michael Gillespie Collection)*

January 1980

At the end of the *Divine Madness* run on Broadway, a stressed-out Bette unceremoniously fires the Harlettes.

February 1980

The attorney for the Harlettes brings a lawsuit against Bette and the Ladd Company (the production company for the film version of *Divine Madness*), claiming that they had been wrongfully terminated, as they had been contracted to be in the *Divine Madness* movie. The singers would eventually win a judgment against Bette and the Ladd Company.

February 15, 1980

The Rose soundtrack is released.

February 22, 1980

Barbara Walters interviewed Bette for the first time in 1980. (ABC)

At the Hollywood Foreign Press Association Golden Globe Awards, Bette wins two awards: one as Best Female Newcomer and another as Best Actress in a Musical/Comedy—*The Rose*.

March 1980
For three days, director Michael Ritchie films Bette on stage for the movie version of *Divine Madness* at the Pasadena Civic Center in California. Despite horrendous weather and Bette being sick with a 103-degree temperature, the filming goes off without incident.

April 1980
Simon and Schuster releases Bette's fanciful—and mostly fictional—memoir of her world tour, *A View From a Broad.*

April 14, 1980
At the Academy Awards, Bette competes for Best Actress for *The Rose* against Jill Clayburgh *(Starting Over)*, Sally Field *(Norma Rae)*, Marsha Mason *(Chapter Two),* and Jane Fonda *(The China Syndrome)*. Bette attends with Peter Riegert, but is crushed when presenter Richard Dreyfuss announces the winner is Sally Field. The same night, Bette appears on *The Barbara Walters Special.*

May 1980
Bette appears in bookstores—complete with a hat designed to look like a typewriter on her head—to sign copies of *A View From a Broad.* In Los Angeles, she signs fifteen hundred copies in three and a half hours, enough to set a record in *The Guiness Book of World Records.*

September 1980
Divine Madness, the movie, opens in U.S. theaters.

November 3, 1980
The *Divine Madness* soundtrack is released.

February 25, 1981
Bette wins a Grammy as Best Female Vocalist for her single of "The Rose," beating Barbra Streisand ("Woman in Love"), Olivia Newton-John ("Magic"), Irene Cara ("Fame"), and Donna Summer ("On the Radio"). Bette's recording of "The Rose" was also nominated as the Record of the Year (losing to "Sailing" by Christopher Cross). Also, as part of *In Harmony: A Sesame Street Record,* Bette wins another Grammy for Best Recording for Children.

May 5, 1981
Bette begins shooting *Jinxed,* costarring Ken Wahl and directed by Don Siegel.

September 1981

Reports in the Hollywood trades and the *Los Angeles Times* paint *Jinxed* as a jinxed production. Ken Wahl and Don Siegel both attack Bette for the problems in making the film, tainting the picture before it even opens.

October 22, 1981

Jinxed opens nationwide, garnering the worst reviews of Bette's film career.

March 29, 1982

Bette is the high point of a generally dull Oscar show, playfully lampooning all five nominees for Best Song before announcing the winner ("Arthur's Theme" from *Arthur*).

November 1982

Bette begins plans for a new concert tour—*De Tour*, a New Wave, artsy, prop-laden musical extravaganza.

December 6, 1982

De Tour commences, with plans to travel to nineteen U.S. cities.

December 31, 1982

In Los Angeles, Bette's on stage in *De Tour* for New Year's Eve. At midnight, she comes out in a diaper with a 1983 sash across her chest. Barry Manilow makes a surprise appearance as Father Time. Together, they greet the new year and lead the audience in "Auld Lang Syne."

March 21, 1983

De Tour ends.

Spring 1983

A depressed, exhausted Bette decides to take time off entirely from performing. She goes to Europe for a while, spends time partying, and returns to New York. Years later, Bette recalls, "I had a nervous breakdown. It's a horrible thing to lose faith in oneself . . . a killer. I sat home crying, sleeping, and spent plenty of time getting drunk on Courvoisier. Finally, I went to a therapist and learned I wasn't to blame, that my feelings of persecution were correct."

May 1983

Bette joins stars Lauren Bacall, Debbie Reynolds, Carol Channing, Harry Belafonte, and others at a benefit for the Actors Fund, a salute to New York's Palace Theater.

August 1, 1983

No Frills, Bette's New Wave–influenced studio album, is released.

September 10–11, 1983

Bette tapes *Art or Bust!*— her name for the *De Tour* TV special—at the Northrup Auditorium, University of Minnesota.

November 1983

Bette appears at a Manhattan Barnes & Noble bookstore to sign copies of her second book, *The Saga of Baby Divine.* It's a children's story about a divine little baby girl who wants "more" out of life.

February 1984

Bette attends a screening of "Beast of Burden," her music video with Mick Jagger.

September 1984

Bette meets Martin von Haselberg. Though they had previously been introduced, Martin—also known as Harry Kipper of the performance art group the Kipper Kids—had lost her number and never asked her out. They begin dating immediately.

December 16, 1984

Although they have not known each other very long, Bette marries Martin von Haselberg (a.k.a. Harry Kipper). They go to Las Vegas and are married in the Candlelight Chapel by a guy who moonlights as an Elvis impersonator.

January 28, 1985

Following the broadcast of the American Music Awards, forty-five stars gather in a Hollywood recording studio to make a record to raise money for famine relief in Ethiopia. Bette joins Bruce Springsteen, Tina Turner, Lionel Richie, Michael Jackson, Cyndi Lauper, and others to perform "We Are the World."

Bette had little reason to smile once **Jinxed** *was released.*

April 1, 1985

"We Are the World" is released as a single and album, quickly rising to the top of the *Billboard* charts.

April 30–May 1, 1985

At the Improvisation in Los Angeles, Bette records material for her first—and, thus far, only—comedy album, *Mud Will Be Flung Tonight!* Aside from Soph jokes, breast jokes, and a little singing, Bette also pokes fun at the making of "We Are the World," and her part in it.

May 20, 1985

Down and Out in Beverly Hills begins shooting.

August 1985

Down and Out wraps production. Disney is high on the project and contemplates a long-term deal for Bette.

September 1985

Bette is given a production deal at Disney. She and partners Margaret Jennings South and Bonnie Bruckheimer form All Girl Productions and begin developing film projects. In 1989, Bette will reflect on their partnership, saying, "All three of us had been on pictures, but had never actually made a picture."

November 1, 1985

Mud Will Be Flung Tonight!, Bette's first comedy album, is released.

November 3, 1985

Bette takes part in *The Best of the Best: A Show of Concern,* a fund-raiser to combat AIDS.

January 1986

Bette visited stores and autographed copies for both her books.

Once Disney executives settle on Bette rather than Madonna for the lead in *Ruthless People,* filming begins in Los Angeles. She signs a long-term deal with Disney.

February 27, 1986

At the second annual Moving Picture Ball, the American Cinemathèque (a Los Angeles film society) honors Bette Midler for her versatile talents in music, drama, and comedy in the theater, TV, and motion pictures. Melissa Manchester, Whoopi Goldberg, and Stevie Wonder, among others, take part in the salute to Bette.

Spring 1986

Bette and costar Shelley Long begin filming *Outrageous Fortune.*

March 31, 1986

Bette announces that she's pregnant with her first child.

May 1986

Fred Midler dies of heart disease.

June 27, 1986

Ruthless People opens nationwide.

September 6, 1986

Bette and Martin are among the dozens of Hollywood stars and civic leaders who attend Barbra Streisand's *One Voice* concert at her Malibu ranch to raise money for the Democratic Party.

November 14, 1986

Bette and Martin von Haselberg's first and only child, Sophie Frederica Alohilani von Haselberg, is born at 8:45 P.M. in Los Angeles. She weighs 8 lbs., 11 oz. Sophie is not named for Sophie Tucker, but Frederica is in homage to Bette's father, Fred, and Alohilani is a bow to Bette's Hawaiian roots. It means "bright sky."

December 22, 1986

The 25 Most Intriguing People of '86 issue of *People* magazine includes Bette. As she herself comments, "It was an extraordinary year. I had two hit movies and a baby. The year went from the ridiculous to the sublime, or rather from the ridiculous to the divine, because my little girl is such a doll."

February 1987

Outrageous Fortune opens nationwide.

February 5, 1987

The Quigley box office poll for 1986 is announced. Bette is number six overall, the highest-rated woman in the top ten.

February 17, 1987

At the ShoWest convention of theater owners and exhibitors in Las Vegas, Bette, Robin Williams, and George Carlin entertain the attend-ees and promote their Disney projects. The high point is a racy, un-Disneyesque retelling of *Snow White and the Seven Dwarfs* by the comic trio.

April 1987

Bette is on the cover of *Life* magazine.

May 19, 1987

Bette is a big winner at the American Comedy Awards. She is given the Lifetime Achievement Award, as well as Funniest Female in a Motion Picture for her performance in *Ruthless People,* Funniest Record and/or Video for *Mud Will Be Flung Tonight!,* and the overall award for Funniest Female Performer of the Year.

September 1987

Bette and Lily Tomlin shoot scenes for *Big Business* on location in New York City.

February 1988

Bette and costar Barbara Hershey begin shooting *Beaches.* It is the first film for Bette's company, All Girl Productions.

March 19, 1988

Bette Midler's Mondo Beyondo airs on HBO.

April 1988

Bette, who is two and a half months pregnant with her second child, suffers a miscarriage. "It was a blighted ovum. The body was acting as though it were pregnant, but the egg had never been fully fertilized," Bette later explains to Delia Ephron (March 1989, *Redbook*).

June 10, 1988

Big Business opens nationwide.

November 18, 1988

Oliver & Company premieres, with Bette voicing the role of Georgette in the animated feature.

November 22, 1988

The soundtrack for *Beaches* is released.

December 14, 1988

Bette appears on *The Oprah Winfrey Show.*

January 13, 1989
Beaches opens nationwide.

March 1989
According to the Quigley poll, Bette is again in the top ten of box office favorites. She is the only woman on the list, ranked number seven.

January 29, 1990
Stella opens nationwide.

February 20, 1990
At the 32nd Annual Grammy Awards, "Wind Beneath My Wings" wins Best Song and Record of the Year. After winning, Bette tells the press: "This record's my first number one. I had to wait seventeen years for it. I hope I don't have to wait another seventeen."

April 22, 1990
ABC-TV airs *The Earth Day Special.* Bette appears in a sketch as Mother Earth.

June 1990
Scenes From a Mall begins shooting in Connecticut and Los Angeles.

September 25, 1990
Some People's Lives is released.

October 1990
Bette and James Caan begin tap-dancing lessons for their roles in *For the Boys.*

1991
Bette contributes a song to *For Our Children,* a special compilation album to raise money for Pediatric AIDS.

January 16, 1991
While shooting continues on *For the Boys*—using actual army reserves as extras—President George Bush announces Operation Desert Storm.

Bette and Lily Tomlin

Suddenly, the reserves are called into action, and the entire production has to watch them depart. To Bette and the company, it feels like they are living the story of *For the Boys*, entertaining the troops as they go off to war.

February 20, 1991
Bette appears at the Grammys, singing "From a Distance," which has become an anthem for the Gulf War.

March 22, 1991
Scenes From a Mall opens nationwide.

September 1991
Bette is presented the Commitment to Life award from AIDS Project Los Angeles.

November 12, 1991
Two weeks before the film opens, the *For the Boys* soundtrack is released.

November 27, 1991
For the Boys opens.

December 10, 1991
Martha Raye decides to sue Bette Midler and her All Girl Productions over the authorship of *For the Boys*. Raye contends that she gave Bette a twenty-page autobiographical treatment that was the basis for the *For the Boys* screenplay.

December 29, 1991
Bette is nominated for a Golden Globe for her role in *For the Boys* in the category Best Actress—Comedy/Musical. Her competition: Ellen Barkin, *Switch;* Kathy Bates, *Fried Green Tomatoes;* Anjelica Huston, *The Addams Family;* and Michelle Pfeiffer, *Frankie and Johnny.*

January 19, 1992
Bette wins the Golden Globe for Best Actress in a Musical/Comedy for *For the Boys.* Her acceptance speech is very emotional, and a little bitter: "I want to thank the Foreign Press Association for honoring a film when the American public dismissed it."

Winning the Golden Globe for **For the Boys** *was a comfort. (Steve Granitz/Retna Ltd.)*

March 23, 1992

Bette scores another victory, this time in court. Her suit against the advertising company Young & Rubicam claimed that they used a sound-alike vocalist singing "Do You Want to Dance?" to deceive the public into thinking Bette Midler was selling Ford Motor Company automobiles. After seven years in the judicial system, a jury awarded her $400,000 in damages. Upon appeal, the decision is upheld.

April 21, 1992

Showtime TV premieres "Weird Parents" on *Shelley Duvall's Bedtime Stories*. Bette narrates the children's story.

May 21, 1992

Bette guests on the penultimate *Tonight Show with Johnny Carson*. She sings "One for the Road" to Johnny, then—completely impromptu—persuades Johnny to sing with her. They do his favorite song, "Here's That Rainy Day." When they finish singing, a teary-eyed Carson looks up at the audience and says quietly, "You people are seeing one helluva show tonight."

August 31, 1992

Even though Bette is not there to receive it, her appearance on *The Tonight Show with Johnny Carson* is awarded an Emmy at the 44th Annual Emmy Awards.

September 23, 1992

Bette is among dozens of stars and celebrities at "Valentino: Thirty Years of Magic," an anniversary party honoring the famed Italian designer, with all proceeds going to AIDS treatment and research.

October 5, 1992

As the presidential election approaches, Bette lends a hand, taking part in voter registration drives in the Los Angeles area.

May 13, 1993

Bette provides her voice for a cartoon rendering of herself in an episode of *The Simpsons* called "Krusty Gets Kancelled." She does a parody of her legendary appearance on Johnny Carson's goodbye show, crooning with Krusty. The segment also includes a nod to Bette's highway cleanup campaign.

June 1993

Experience the Divine: Bette Midler's Greatest Hits is released.

Summer 1993

Gypsy, Bette's first TV movie, an adaptation of the smash Broadway musical, begins shooting.

August 1993

Bette announces her first concert tour in ten years—*Experience the Divine.* Her reasons for returning to the stage are clear: "Finally, ultimately, I want to be, I want to do, what it is that I do, not what somebody else does. That really is what drove me back on stage. I was just tired of working for other people [in the movies] and trying to drag them into my vision. You get tired of accommodating. I want to open my mouth and have things come out that I intend to say."

September 14, 1993

Experience the Divine opens a record-setting engagement at Radio City Music Hall in New York. Because of the incredible demand, the initial ten shows are doubled, then tripled. In the history of Radio City Music Hall, she becomes the only artist ever to play thirty shows in a single engagement.

September 15, 1993

Jule Styne, composer of *Gypsy,* attends Bette's Radio City concert. She asks him to stand and accept the acknowledgment of the crowd, then dedicates her performance of "Rose's Turn" to him.

November 9, 1993

The *Gypsy* soundtrack is released.

December 12, 1993

Gypsy premieres on CBS-TV. The Midler production is lauded by the critics and scores well in the Nielsens.

December 15, 1993

New York's Radio City Music Hall unveils its "Sidewalk of Stars," honoring fourteen stars, including Bette Midler, Liza Minnelli, Tina Turner, and Frank Sinatra.

December 21, 1993

The *Experience the Divine* tour is rated one of the top-grossing U.S. road shows, according to *Performance* magazine. She rakes in $18.8 million in fifty shows.

January 10, 1994

In Oakland, California, as part of a police action to get people to turn in illegal guns, one of the items offered in exchange for the guns is tickets to a Bette Midler concert.

January 24, 1994

All Girl Productions signs Chevy Chase to star in *Pals Forever* (later changed to *Man of the House*) for Disney.

January 25, 1994

At the Golden Globe Awards, Bette receives a statuette for her performance as Mama Rose in the TV movie *Gypsy*. She is not there to receive it, though. She is with her family on vacation in Hawaii following the horrendous L.A. earthquake.

February 16, 1994

Bette appears in a Los Angeles courtroom to deny that *For the Boys* was based on the life of Martha Raye, who had brought a suit in 1991 against Bette's All Girl Productions and 20th Century Fox claiming they had used Raye's story for the picture. "The stories have no resemblance except for one thing—they both were entertainers during wartime," Bette testifies, when asked about the source material for the script. The court rules in Bette's favor.

February 18, 1994

Gypsy is released on home video.

Spring–Summer 1994

Bette decides to take *Experience the Divine* back out on the road. Bette tells the *Boston Globe:* "We had a fabulous time last year. And when the season rolled around again, we decided to do it again. There were a whole bunch of places we didn't get to last year, and there were requests to come back to some of the places we did get to, so we

Bette's Radio City show was the biggest thing in New York. (Joseph Marzullo/Retna Ltd.)

strapped on the old harness and here we are again."

Fall 1994

Bette, Martin, and Sophie move from California back to New York City, getting a loft in TriBeCa. "I moved back because of the earthquake. And I needed to get back to a town where I could have a conversation about something other than grosses," she will tell Stephen Holden of the *New York Times* in 1995.

September 11, 1994

At the 46th Annual Emmy Awards, Bette opens the show with a dazzling live rendition of "Rose's Turn" from *Gypsy*. Although she is nominated for Outstanding Actress in a TV Movie/Special, Bette loses to Kirstie Alley *(David's Mother)*. *Gypsy* is also nominated for Outstanding Made-for-TV Movie, losing to the HBO AIDS drama *And the Band Played On.*

October 4, 1994

The Manhattan Transfer's new album, *Tonin',* is released. Bette guests on the CD, singing "Gonna Take a Miracle" with the group.

January 1995

Bette begins recording sessions for *Bette of Roses.*

March 1995

Bette appears at the White House reception in honor of National Public Radio's twenty-fifth anniversary. In her inimitable style, Bette jokes, "I'm not going to get political. We don't come to the White House for that. We come hoping that there will be embossed towels that we can take home to our family and friends."

May 21, 1995

Bette appears on *Seinfeld* playing herself in an episode called, "The Understudy."

Experience the Divine brought Delores DeLago out of dry-dock. (Michael Gillespie Collection)

June 22, 1995

Bette is honored by VH1 for the charitable efforts on behalf of the Manhattan Restoration Project in New York. She sings "To Deserve

You," then joins country singer Wynonna Judd for "Let It Be Me."

July 11, 1995
Bette of Roses, Bette's first non-film-related album in years, is released. It is also her last studio project for Atlantic Records. After being with the label for twenty-three years, she announces that she is moving to Warner Bros. Records.

October 20, 1995
Get Shorty opens. It features Bette in a small, unbilled, but brilliant comic turn.

February 11, 1996
At the American Comedy Awards, Bette Midler, John Travolta, and Dennis Farina are all winners for their roles in *Get Shorty*. Even though her role is an extended cameo, Bette is named Funniest Supporting Female.

September 20, 1996
The First Wives Club, starring Bette, Goldie Hawn, and Diane Keaton, opens.

December 3, 1996
Bette Midler launches a multi-city West Coast concert tour at the Orange County Performing Arts Center. The show is a revised and revamped *Experience the Divine*, now called *Diva Las Vegas* in anticipation of her HBO TV special that will be filmed at the MGM Grand Garden in Las Vegas.

December 23, 1996
Bette's *Diva Las Vegas* show plays the Universal Amphitheater in Los Angeles, getting rave reviews.

January 10–11, 1997
The cameras roll taping Bette's *Diva Las Vegas* show for broadcast on HBO.

January 18, 1997
Diva Las Vegas, Bette's HBO TV special, premieres.

Bette, Goldie, and Diane filmed **The First Wives Club** *in Manhattan. (Bill Davila/Retna Ltd.)*

THREE

Who's Who and What's What in the World of Bette Midler

Adopt-a-Highway

One of Bette's pet charities. In 1995, in New York, she donated $2,000 a month to pay for the cleanup and beautification of sections of the Bronx River Parkway. In 1991, Bette had adopted a stretch of the Ventura Freeway in Los Angeles for similar antilitter and cleanup activities.

All Girl Productions

The film production company Bette created in 1985 with partners Bonnie Bruckheimer and Margaret Jennings South. Their motto is "We Hold a Grudge."

Amsel, Richard

A gifted commercial artist whose provocative and amusing artwork of Bette was used to illustrate her earliest music engagements, including her first two album covers.

Baby Divine

A character Bette created, in her own image, as the heroine of her children's book, *The Saga of Baby Divine*.

Bette mocked her role in **The Greatest Story Ever Overtold** *for her book* **A View From a Broad.**

"Beast of Burden"

Rolling Stone song written by Mick Jagger and Keith Richards for the 1978 *Some Girls* album. Bette did a duet of it with Jagger for her *No Frills* album, and it was also filmed as a music video with Bette and Mick as cantankerous lovers whose shenanigans are plastered all over the tabloids. The video was shot at New York's Peppermint Lounge dance club.

Blatt, Jerry

One of Bette's best friends and most important cocreators. He knew Bette better than most people, and said of her in 1987, "She couples incredible toughness with great softness. You feel she could creak, crumble at any minute." In 1991, when Bette was asked about going back on the concert stage, she recalled Blatt: "I think about [returning to the stage] all the time. But my best friend and collaborator, Jerry Blatt, died of AIDS a couple of years ago, and he was so irreplaceable. When we didn't have a big fancy production, we had to rely on wit and cleverness. . . . It was so much fun, and now that he is gone, I just don't know if it would be the same experience, if I could ever find anyone to come up to his standards."

Bruckheimer, Bonnie

One of Bette's business partners in All Girl Productions. She worked with directors Paul Schrader and Arthur Penn before becoming Aaron Russo's assistant on *The Rose,* and then Bette's business partner. Aside from being associates, Bonnie—a Brooklyn-born divorced mother of two, who was formerly married to producer Jerry Bruckheimer—and Bette are close friends. Bette is godmother to one of Bonnie's kids, and Bonnie is Sophie's godmother.

Mick Jagger collaborated with Bette for "Beast of Burden."

Candlelight Wedding Chapel, the

The site of Martin and Bette's December 16, 1985, Las Vegas wedding. According to Bette, "We checked into the wedding suite at Caesar's Palace. I was wearing a grayish blue chiffon, it cost a fortune, but I really wanted to impress [Martin]. My dress was very boom-boom, it had strings of beads hanging down, I made a nice racket walking down the aisle. It was 2 A.M., we got our license and wound up at the Candlelight Wedding Chapel. We put on a soundtrack of Fellini's *Juliet of the Spirits,* got teary-eyed. The guy who read the ceremony was an Elvis impersonator." Bette has said of her husband, "He sees to the heart of things. He respects and supports what I do, and he leads me, too, when I lose my way."

Carson, Johnny

The former host of *The Tonight Show,* he was one of Bette's earliest and most ardent supporters. To show Johnny her thanks, Bette appeared on his next-to-last show, singing his favorite song—"Here's That Rainy Day"—with him, crooning "One for My Baby (And One More for the Road)" to him, and reminiscing about their shared past. Bette's appearance was so memorable, she won an Emmy for it.

Carousel

The classic Rodgers and Hammerstein musical was the very first theatrical production Bette saw, at age twelve. She knew then that she had to become an actress. "I couldn't get over how beautiful it was. I fell so in love with it. Everything else in my life receded once I discovered theater."

Continental Baths, The

The New York City gay bathhouse that Stuart Ostrow converted into a nightclub and multi-entertainment spot in 1972. Bette, who had been singing at small clubs like Hilly's, was booked into the club and caused a sensation with her singing and joking. The place became the launching pad for Bette Midler, and in Bette's tour memoir, *A View From a Broad,* she joked that no matter what she accomplishes in her career, she will always have the label "began career at Continental Baths." Still, Bette was very grateful for the opportunity the tubs afforded her: "Me and those boys, we just went somewhere else. It was so much fun. I had the best time. It was something I just had to do, and I did it for them, and I did it all. And I must say, they probably saw the most inspired of it. It was really abandon. I did some crap, I did some good stuff, and I

Iris Rainer Dart created C.C. Bloom in **Beaches** *for Bette.*

learned a lot," she told Chris Chase in the *New York Times*. Bette lovingly refers to the Continental Baths as "the tubs."

Dart, Iris Rainer

The author of *Beaches*, Dart created the character of C.C. Bloom with Bette Midler in mind. According to Bette, "Iris always thought I had a lot of energy and heart and she wanted to write me something with music in the area of *The Rose*. . . . I know she wrote [*Beaches*] for me, but I don't know that my life informed what she wrote. Until she met me, she always believed that I was a larger-than-life kind of personality. We tried very hard to make the characters—warts and all—not just identifiable, but people that you could like, or even have over for dinner. I think she wanted to create a part that had those old-fashioned elements."

DeMora, Bob

Costume and set designer whom Bette calls "a genius." Among his designs were Delores DeLago's mermaid costume and the Harlette waitress dresses that opened to American flags.

Disney

American film studio where Bette reclaimed her film career after the disastrous *Jinxed* fiasco. Bette signed a long-term deal with the studio, and was its most popular star in the mid-1980s.

The Divine Miss M

The alter ego Bette created for her first musical engagements. For a while, the world was under the impression that Bette was the Divine Miss M and no one else, a misconception Bette put to rest with her second album, *Bette Midler*. "That's the only character that I ever made up

by myself. I made her up out of whole cloth. I was in New York, I saw these people, I looked at these movies, I said, 'This is what I want to be.' And that's what I became. That's what I made up. But then I didn't want to get stuck in it."

DeLago, Delores

The "Toast of Chicago," a truly tacky mermaid, confined to a motorized wheelchair, who specializes in lounge lizard music and Polynesian ball twirling. She's been a feature in most of Bette's concerts, including *Divine Madness* and *Experience the Divine.* According to Bette's 1980 tour program, Vicki Eydie, her original incarnation of a lounge singer, metamorphosed into Delores.

With Disney chief Michael Eisner, Bette helped open the Disney MGM Park in Orlando.

Daly, Tyne

Tony winner for the role of Mama Rose in the 1990 Broadway revival of *Gypsy*. Daly, a four-time Emmy winner, was incensed when she was passed over for the TV version of *Gypsy*. She told *TV Guide,* "I feel like I've been punched in the face. I read about the decision in the papers like everybody else. Midler is a great power and a great entity, but there's a bigger and larger power moderating here, and it's called money."

Eydie, Vicki

The ultimate bad lounge singer, a creation of Bette's who appeared in *The Fabulous Bette Midler* HBO TVspecial, as well as on the *Live at Last* album. She was the star of her very own global revue, *Around the World in Eighty Ways*. Eventually, Vicki became Delores DeLago.

Gillespie, Ben

Bette with the Staggering Harlettes during Clams on the Half-Shell *(Michael Gillespie Collection)*

Bette's first mentor, he was a dancer in *Fiddler on the Roof* when Bette was in the chorus. Ben encouraged Bette's singing and exposed her to all kinds of music and theater. "He introduced me to the world. He played records for me, we went to old movies together, we talked about art. I worshipped him. I was with him for three years and he literally changed my life. He made me want to sing. . . . I'd never taken a music class, couldn't read music, didn't know what to listen to. [Ben] played me the blues, Bessie Smith records, played me Ruth Etting, Aretha Franklin, Morgana King, Ike and Tina Turner. He took me someplace every night—I even heard Janis Joplin at the Fillmore East."

Greatest Story Ever Overtold, The

A low-budget, experimental satire about the Christ story, with Bette cast as the Virgin Mary. It was made in 1971 in Canada, directed by Peter Alexander, and was a complete flop. In 1974, producers renamed it *The Divine Mr. J* and tried to get the film re-released in New York City to take advantage of Bette's burgeoning stardom. Bette's manager at the time, Aaron Russo, fought the release, claiming that the advertising—promoting Bette as the star—was misleading. Russo managed to get the producers to change the ads, and his publicity campaign denouncing the movie was enough to ward off Midler fans. The film was later released on home video as *The Thorn*.

Harlettes, the Staggering

Bette's backup singer-dancers. The Harlettes—dozens of different girls over the years—have backed Bette since her very earliest concerts. "I was very inspired by Tina Turner," Bette recalled in 1997. "I saw her at the Fillmore and she had the most unbelievable group of backup singers that I ever saw in my life and I never really recovered from it. When I first started singing, I had no backup singers and I always felt that they would fill in the blanks. So I thought about it for a long time—and had a few drinks—then I decided that I wanted to call them the Harlettes, 'cause I wanted something that would be a little racy, but I didn't want to be insulting to anybody. . . . I've had wonderful, wonderful girls behind me. They were all soloists in their own right. All stars. They all deserved to be in front." Among the Harlettes of note were Melissa Manchester, Katey Sagal, Jenifer Lewis, and Linda Hart. In 1996, comedienne-writer Lisa Amsterdam was working on a TV series called *The Harlettes,* for CBS, which will be produced by Bette and Bonnie Bruckheimer for All Girl Productions.

Hawaii

The movie, not the state. Bette was cast in the George Roy Hill film version of James Michener's bestseller while she was still a student at the University of Hawaii. She played a missionary's wife and had no lines; in fact, only an eagle-eyed viewer can catch her in the early ship scenes. Still, *Hawaii* was a very important film in Bette's life. When the company moved from Hawaii to Los Angeles to finish filming, Bette was taken along. "I made $300 a week, and $70 per diem. I ate on $2 a day. When it was over, I had all the money," Bette told Chris Chase in the *New York Times*. She used the money to move to New York City and begin her career on the stage.

Hennessy, Bill

Bette's first talent manager, he was one of the most important influences on Bette's life. He helped write her first concert acts.

Hoffman, Dustin

Oscar-winning actor who appeared as a guest on Bette's first prime-time network TV special, the Emmy Award–winning *Ol' Red Hair Is Back*. He played the piano and accompanied Bette on the song "Shoot the Breeze," which they had written together.

Layton, Joe

Choreographer-director who directed many of Bette's stage shows, including the *Clams on the Half-Shell Revue* and *Experience the Divine*. Layton also worked with Barbra Streisand on her Emmy-winning TV specials. When *Diva Las Vegas* (a revised *Experience the Divine*) was broadcast on HBO, Bette dedicated it to Joe, who had passed away the year before.

Lottery, The

The short film in which Bette appears that plays at the MGM Disney World attraction as part of the Great Movie Tour. The feature presents Bette as a music teacher who wins the lottery. Before she can cash in the ticket, it flies out the window of her apartment and is taken away by a bird. To get the ticket back, Bette has to climb out on a ledge, ends up falling onto a pushcart in the street, and then careens into a subway station, nearly crashing into an oncoming train! The film is then dissected piece by piece to explain the tricks of filmmaking.

Manilow, Barry

A very popular singer-composer, Manilow began his career as a jingle writer and accompanist. When Bette first made a splash at the Continental Baths, Barry was her pianist. He became her arranger and conductor, helping to shape her music. Manilow coproduced Bette's first two albums and toured with Bette until 1973. In the last tour,

Barry conducted the band, but also performed a set on his own to promote his debut album. He and Bette parted company professionally when Manilow's solo career took off. They have remained good friends and occasionally get together socially.

Mardin, Arif

Record producer and senior vice president of Atlantic Records, Mardin has been the guiding force in Bette's recording career. Their relationship dates back to the very beginning of her career: Mardin was an arranger on *The Divine Miss M* and coproduced *Bette Midler*. Mardin also produced the albums *Beaches*, *Some People's Lives*, and *Bette of Roses*, three of Bette's biggest sellers. Bette has said of him: "Arif's a real character. He's a great, great musician, and I have tremendous respect for him. I think he enjoys working with me because I bring him different kinds of songs to work with—songs that are a little off the beaten path, where he can really stretch his arranging wings. He also has such patience with me because, of course, I'm insane."

Midler Family, the

Bette's mother was born Ruth Schindel and raised in Paterson, New Jersey. Her father, Fred—nicknamed Chesty because he was a body builder—was also from Paterson. Bette's father fell in love with Hawaii while in the navy, moving his family there before Bette's birth in 1945. Fred and Ruth had four children: Susan (named for Susan Hayward), Judith (named for Judy Garland), Bette (named for Bette Davis), and a son, Daniel. Daniel suffered brain damage as an infant, but it is thanks to Fred that he was able to learn how to read and write and take care of himself. "Every afternoon [he taught Danny]. None of us wanted to be in the house, but Daniel did learn, and it's made a big difference in his life. It gave him freedom," Bette recalled. As an adult,

Long after working together, Bette and Barry Manilow have remained good friends. (Steve Granitz/Retna Ltd.)

Daniel has a job, lives alone, and is self-sufficient. Susan has become a health care executive in New York City. Judy died in 1968, while visiting Bette in New York. "She was walking along 44th Street, a car came out of a garage and killed her. I was the only family member in town. I had to go to the morgue and identify the body. I don't think my mother ever recovered from the shock." Bette described her mother as her greatest supporter. "She thought I could do no wrong. . . . My mother was, oh, stunning, and very hardworking. She sewed beautifully. She made all our clothes for years, until my parents discovered the Salvation Army. We were really poor." Fred Midler, on the other hand, was very down on Bette's career, even after she became a success. Bette remembered how he was when she was growing up: "He was a bit of a tyrant. He would flush the girls' makeup down the toilet. He'd lock Susan out of the house when she came home too late. . . . He never chose to see me perform, except on Johnny Carson. He said I looked like a loose woman." Ruth Midler died in 1979 of leukemia and liver and breast cancer; Fred died from heart disease in May 1986.

Pieridine Three, the
The folksinging group Bette formed with two other girls while she was still at Radford High School in Honolulu. In 1995, while promoting *Bette of Roses,* her sixteenth album, Bette remembered the Pieridine Three: "I was actually a folksinger when I first started out. I had a little vocal trio and we did Peter, Paul, and Mary covers. I guess I'm dating myself, but I really do love the hopefulness and spirit of folk music. I also have a strong affinity to country music, which I picked up as a kid and never really lost."

Raye, Martha
Legendary comedienne who claimed that *For the Boys* was based on her life story. She sued All Girl Productions in 1992, saying that she gave Bette a twenty-page autobiographical treatment based on her USO experience, and was not paid for it. Bette's company contended that the story was a work of fiction, and the court ruled in Bette's favor.

Riegert, Peter
Talented actor in films as diverse as *Animal House* and *Crossing Delancey,* he was Bette's boyfriend from 1976 to 1980. In 1993, she chose him to be her leading man in the TV movie adaptation of *Gypsy.* In 1977, Bette told *New York,* "He and I have a relationship that's utterly painless. We're great companions—we keep each other company, and we

lift each other up when we're down, and it's very simple and straight-forward. There's none of the game crap between us. . . . I love to talk to him and look at him and I think I even understand him. . . . I can see why people get married now that I have Pete."

Rivera, Geraldo

The talk show host and journalist who wrote about his brief, steamy sexual encounter with Bette in his memoir, *Exposing Myself.* Bette went ballistic over Rivera's account of their 1972 fling, especially when he labeled her as sexually insatiable. Bette told ABC newswoman Barbara Walters that he had drugged and groped her during an interview in her Greenwich Village apartment. In 1991, Rivera admitted that he regretted writing the book. "I should have waited until I was sixty to do the book. Maybe people would have been less offended."

Russo, Aaron

Perhaps the most influential man in Bette Midler's life . . . up until 1979, when they parted company. Russo became Midler's manager in 1972, when Bette asked him to make her a legend and he agreed. They had a brief love affair, which complicated their working relation-ship. Although Russo was a master manipulator and often played "head games" with Bette, he was also extremely loyal and wanted the biggest and best for her. Right before their split, Bette told the *Sunday New York Times:* "Many people think our relationship is unhealthy. As a matter of fact, most of them do. But Aaron thinks I'm the greatest thing that ever walked, and he did when nobody else did. He's not per-sonally graceful, but he does what he thinks is best for me. Sometimes he's wrong, but most of the time he's right. I'm the only person he has. Who else is there on the market who has that? I consider myself lucky to have someone who devotes all his energies and time to my career. Why would I dump that? . . . We play pretty terrible games with each other, but in its way, it's a good relationship." However, the rela-tionship was destined to fail. In the November 14, 1983, *People,* Bette revealed what happened during the 1979 Broadway run of *Bette Midler: Divine Madness* that ended their collaboration: "Aaron had a mythic obsession with me. I wanted to be free, and he wanted me to be his. [He came to see the show and] . . . told me it was a terrible show. He said I was ruining all he had done for me and that I looked like an albino on stage. When he told me this, I was sick with bronchitis. I had my head in the toilet, barfing. Aaron always did know my weakest moments, and then he would strike. After that, I never saw him again."

Rydell, Mark

Film director who guided Bette to two of her most memorable screen characterizations, Rose in *The Rose* and Dixie in *For the Boys.* Both roles earned Bette Academy Award nominations.

Shabba-Doo

Dancer who made it big during the early 1980s break-dancing craze. In 1978, Shabba-Doo toured with Bette. "She gave me my first per-sonal break as an artist. We played Broadway. I guess I was the first person to bring street dancing to the legitimate stage. We played the Majestic Theater in her *Divine Madness* show."

"Silent Night"

The very first song Bette performed before an audience—in first grade. She won a prize, although as a Jew she felt guilty singing a Christmas carol.

Simon, Paul

Top recording star and award-winning singer-composer, he had a brief affair with Bette in 1975. They were to record "Gone at Last" as a duet, but things didn't work out. Simon ended up doing the record with Phoebe Snow. Bette was baffled, but Aaron Russo took the blame, admitting that the problems between Columbia Records (Simon's label) and Atlantic (Bette's label) were exacerbated by him because he was jealous of Bette's feelings for Simon.

Soph

A Bette character, originally inspired by singer Sophie Tucker, who is now a staple of every Midler concert. Soph is the teller of extremely bawdy, racy jokes about herself, her boyfriend Ernie, and her girl-friend Clementine.

Team Disney

The Tuscan-style office building—with statuary depicting each of the seven dwarfs—on the Disney Studio lot in California, which is referred to as "the House That Bette Built." In Kevin Sessum's December 1991 *Vanity Fair* article, he explains that the nearly $300 million the studio earned on Midler movies—*Down and Out in Beverly Hills, Ruthless People, Outrageous Fortune, Big Business, Beaches, Stella,* and *Scenes From a Mall*—helped finance the new building.

Titsling, Otto

The inventor of the first brassiere, you know, "the over-the-shoulder boulder holder!" According to Bette, she was told a story about Titsling inventing the breast support and having a French designer—Phillipe de Brassiere—steal the concept and get a patent. So moved by the story was Bette that she wrote a song about it. The song (cowritten with Jerry Blatt, Marc Shaiman, and Charlene Seeger) first debuted on *Mud Will Be Flung Tonight!* and was the basis of a musical number in *Beaches*.

Vilanch, Bruce

One of Bette's chief collaborators, he has helped write almost all of her shows. He is also responsible for many of the Soph jokes. He first saw Bette perform when he was writing for the *Chicago Tribune:* "She came out from the kitchen and she was wearing a shirt with no bra. This was the beginning of the women's lib movement. It was a political statement not to wear a bra, but in Bette's case it was a terrorist act! . . . She came out singing 'Sha-Boom,' which was her opening number, and shaking everything she had. All through the room you could hear forks dropping and people choking on ice cubes. Then she did this incredible torch song, 'Remember My Forgotten Man.' She was every diva I had ever loved rolled into one. Plus, it was the most eclectic musical presentation I'd ever seen one person do. She spanned every style and every decade."

Long after their affair, Peter Riegert and Bette teamed up in Gypsy. *(CBS)*

von Haselberg, Martin

Bette's husband, the only man to whom she's ever been married. He is an English-educated, German-born, Buenos Aires–raised man who is also known as Harry Kipper, half of the Kipper Kids, a performance art duo. Martin has also been a commodities broker and, more recently, studied filmmaking at the American Film Institute.

von Haselberg, Sophie Frederica Alohilani

Bette's daughter and only child, born November 14, 1986. She was not named for Sophie Tucker. Frederica was in homage to Bette's father, Fred. Alohilani was a nod to Bette's Hawaiian upbringing; it means "bright sky," "and I hope Sophie has it every day. She deserves it." When Sophie was a toddler, Bette said of her, "I adore her. Her face swims before me when she's not there, and I think about her before I go to sleep at night and I dream about her, and I wake up and I can't wait to see her." More recently—1995—Bette revealed, "She looks a lot like me: she has the smile, she has my eyes, she has my hair. And she's sharp as a tack. She's very funny—her impersonations are some of the best I've ever heard." In the *Diva Las Vegas* TV special, Sophie can be spotted as part of the chorus in the "Ukelele Lady" sequence.

"Wig Song"

A little ditty that Bette composed and sang for her toddler daughter, Sophie. It goes like this: "Oh you gotta wear a wig-wig-wig-wig-wig if you're gonna be famous, you gotta wear a wig-wiggety-wig-wiggety-wig if you're gonna be smart. Because a wig will hide the worst of all your features. Yes, a wig will really help you play the part!"

Young & Rubicam

The advertising agency that used a singer to imitate Bette's recording of "Do You Want to Dance?" for a Ford Motor Company commercial. Bette sued and won a landmark judgment against them. After they appealed the decision, Bette won $400,000 in damages. In 1991, Bette commented, "I think the whole idea of Madison Avenue taking popular music is really loathsome in the first place. I think it's like taking your culture and turning it into something used only to sell stuff. And I'm a snob: I don't buy anything that's advertised on television, just to be mean and ornery."

A combustible combination: Aaron Russo and Bette

FOUR

*F*or the Record

"She was a made-to-order fantasy. She was unlike anybody I'd seen before. People of all types—grandmothers, couples, drag queens—everyone was screaming and jumping up and down on tables for this woman. She was doing everything. . . . You could discern a great wit there—she was trying to seem raunchy and tasteless and exude a certain elegance, and she pulled it off. What she had was style!"

—AHMET ERTEGUN, PRESIDENT, ATLANTIC RECORDS

"Music is something that I just have always had to do and wanted to do and loved to do." That's what Bette Midler said in 1995 about her recording career. Bette has also referred to her checkered musical success as "the Scud missile of show business." And while you may think it's odd for a multi-award-winning singer to regard her work with such skepticism, it is true that the magic of Bette Midler has never been captured in the recording studio. However, there have been moments—brilliant, incredible, and memorable ones—that have characterized her sixteen albums. Here is a recap of the divine musical legacy of America's finest concert performer.

Bette burst on the record industry with her debut album, **The Divine Miss M.**

*Altogether, Bette has won
four Grammys for her music.*

The Divine Miss M

ORIGINALLY RELEASED AS ATLANTIC #7238

NOVEMBER 7, 1972

(Atlantic Remastered Series CD #82785-2)

Produced by Joel Dorn, Barry Manilow,
Geoffrey Haslam,
and Ahmet Ertegun

Do You Want to Dance?
Chapel of Love
Superstar
Daytime Hustler
Am I Blue?
Friends
Hello in There
Leader of the Pack
Delta Dawn
Boogie Woogie Bugle Boy
Friends

Highest position on *Billboard* Top 200: #9
Status: Platinum

Bette dedicated this, her debut album, to her sister Judith, who had died in 1968. She also thanked, among others, "Fred & Ruth, Susie & Danny," i.e., her parents, sister and brother.

Barry Manilow, Melissa Manchester, and Cissy Houston provided background vocals for Bette. At the time, Manchester was a Harlette. Merle Miller and Gail Kantor—the other two Harlettes at the time—are also heard providing backup.

"Do You Want to Dance?" was released as a single, January 20, 1973. It reached #17 on the *Billboard* Top 100. "Boogie Woogie Bugle Boy" was released off the album on June 8, 1973. It reached a high of #8 in *Billboard*. On November 10, 1973, a third single from the album, "Friends," was released. It was on the *Billboard* chart for only a week and ranked #40.

Commenting on the album, Mike Jan of *Cue* magazine, wrote: "Considering the spectacularly funny nature of her career thus far, she would have been forgiven for seizing the opportunity to goof off on the record, to present ten or twelve puffy parodies of old rock songs and popular songs from the thirties and forties, and that would be it. Few probably expected more. Yet Miss Midler has provided much more. Half of the album's ten songs are ballads. Nobody opens her recording career with five ballads without shooting for vocal respectability. Miss Midler clearly is and for it she richly deserves praise. . . . 'Hello in There,' the high point of the second side, is a John Prine song about an aged couple, a recent classic which Miss Midler handles splendidly. *The Divine Miss M* is a fine first album; it could have been better, were it not for the decision to simulate her stage show and include the beastly with the beautiful."

Bette Midler

ORIGINALLY RELEASED AS ATLANTIC #7270
NOVEMBER 16, 1973

(Atlantic Remastered Series CD #82779-2)

Produced by Arif Mardin and Barry Manilow

Skylark
Drinking Again
Breaking Up Somebody's Home
Surabaya Johnny
I Shall Be Released
Optimistic Voices/Lullaby of Broadway
In the Mood
Uptown/Don't Say Nothin' Bad (About My Baby)
/Da Doo Run Run
Twisted
Higher and Higher (Your Love Keeps Lifting Me)

Highest position on *Billboard* Top 200: #6
Status: Gold

Bette dedicated this album to Aaron, the Baron, Russo, her manager at the time. In the thank-yous, she again remembered her parents.

Background vocals included Harlettes old and new: Gale Kantor, Merle Miller, Sharon Redd, Robin Grean, and Charlotte Crossley. Also singing in the background was Barry Manilow, who by this time was under contract to Bell Records (later changed to Arista).

As with her first album, Richard Amsel drew the cover art for *Bette Midler*.

"In the Mood" was the single release from the album. It reached #51 on the *Billboard* chart.

Songs for the New Depression

ORIGINALLY RELEASED AS ATLANTIC #18155 JANUARY 8, 1976

(Atlantic Remastered Series CD #82784-2)

Produced by Moogy Klingman

Strangers in the Night
I Don't Want the Night to End
Mr. Rockefeller
Old Cape Cod
Buckets of Rain
Love Says It's Waiting
Shiver Me Timbers/Samedi et Vendredi
No Jestering
Tragedy
Marahuana
Let Me Just Follow Behind

Highest position on *Billboard* Top 200: #27

The most notable contributor to Bette's third album was Bob Dylan. He joined Bette for a duet on his song "Buckets of Rain." Luther Vandross provided background vocals on "Strangers in the Night." Todd Rundgren played guitar on "I Don't Want the Night to End" and "No Jestering," and sang background on "Let Me Just Follow Behind."

Bette cowrote the lyrics to "Samedi et Vendredi" with Moogy Klingman. Bette also is listed as assistant engineer on the album.

Once again, Bette used the artwork of Richard Amsel, this time on the inner sleeve.

Live at Last

ORIGINALLY RELEASED JUNE 1977

(Atlantic Remastered Series CD #81461-2)

Produced by Lew Hahn
Remote recording produced by Arif Mardin
Recorded live at the Cleveland Music Hall, Cleveland, Ohio,
February 1976

Backstage

Friends/Oh My My

Bang, You're Dead

Birds

Comic Relief

In the Mood

Hurry On Down

Shiver Me Timbers

The Vicki Eydie Show:
a. Around the World; b. Istanbul; c. Fiesta
in Rio; d. South Seas Scene/Hawaiian War Chant;
e. Lullaby of Broadway

Intermission: You're Moving Out Today

Delta Dawn

Long John Blues

Those Wonderful Sophie Tucker Jokes

The Story of Nanette:
a. Nanette; b. Alabama Song/Drinking Again;
c. Mr. Rockefeller; d. Ready to Begin Again
/Do You Want to Dance?

Fried Eggs

Hello in There

Finale:
a. Up the Ladder to the Roof;
b. Boogie Woogie Bugle Boy; c. Friends

Highest position on *Billboard* Top 200: #49

This show is the same one that was recorded for HBO TV as *The Fabulous Bette Midler.*

"You're Moving Out Today" was released as a single, charting to #42 in *Billboard.*

Broken Blossom

ORIGINALLY RELEASED AS ATLANTIC #80410

NOVEMBER 17, 1977

(Atlantic Remastered Series CD #82780-2)

Produced by Brooks Arthur

Make Yourself Comfortable
You Don't Know Me
Say Goodbye to Hollywood
I Never Talk to Strangers
Storybook Children
Red
Empty Bed Blues
A Dream Is a Wish Your Heart Makes
Paradise
Yellow Beach Umbrella
La Vie en Rose

Highest position on *Billboard* Top 200: #51

With **The Rose,** *Bette sank her teeth into rock 'n' roll.*

Tom Waits wrote "I Never Talk to Strangers" and joined Bette for the duet on the album. In the liner notes, Bette wrote: "Dear Waits, Thanks for 'Strangers.' Bette."

Arthur Bell of the *Village Voice* wrote: "*Broken Blossom* is her best, with hardly any camping, and yet it's selling worst of all. But to ask that she stretch, expand, play it straight, is tantamount to suggesting that Muhammad Ali go on a parsley diet. As it stands, Bette is neither middle-of-the-road or far left. She's stuck in a soft shoulder."

"Storybook Children" was released as a single, charting on *Billboard* as high as #57.

Thighs and Whispers

ORIGINALLY RELEASED AS ATLANTIC #16004
AUGUST 24, 1979

(Atlantic Remastered Series CD #82786-2)

Produced by Arif Mardin

Big Noise From Winnetka
Millworker
Cradle Days
My Knight in Black Leather
Hang On in There Baby
Hurricane
Rain
Married Men

Highest position on *Billboard* Top 200: #65

Luther Vandross provided background vocals on several tracks, as did former Harlettes Ula Hedwig, Merle Miller, and Robin Grean. This was the first album to which Marc Shaiman, one of Bette's most significant collaborators, contributed. Bette dedicated this album "For Ruth, my mother."

In the *The Village Voice*, Stephen Holden was unimpressed with *Thighs and Whispers:* "Midler's latest studio album teams her with Arif Mardin, whose elegant pop-soul arrangements obviously scared her to pieces. Though for a change she stays on pitch most of the time, this hard-won precision requires a near-total sacrifice of personality. The best cut, 'Big Noise From Winnetka,' is an arranger's showpiece. The worst, Johnny Bristol's 'Hang On in There Baby,' has Midler sounding like a luded-out Donna Summer, her voice a frightened mew in a swamp of production."

"Married Men" was released on July 7, 1979, as a single. It was on the *Billboard* chart for two weeks, reaching #40.

The haunting title song of **The Rose** *won Bette another Grammy.*

The Rose

ORIGINALLY RELEASED AS ATLANTIC #16010
FEBRUARY 15, 1980

(Atlantic Remastered Series CD #82778-2)

Produced by Paul A. Rothchild

Whose Side Are You On?
Midnight in Memphis
Concert Monologue
When a Man Loves a Woman
Sold My Soul to Rock 'n' Roll
Keep On Rockin'
Love Me With a Feeling
Camillia
Homecoming Monologue
Stay With Me
Let Me Call You Sweetheart
The Rose

Highest position on Billboard Top 200: #12
Status: Double Platinum

The first single off the soundtrack was "When a Man Loves a Woman," released March 1, 1980. It charted in *Billboard* for three weeks, reaching #35. On April 26, 1980, the title song—"The Rose"—was released. It charted for sixteen weeks and reached #3, according to *Billboard*. The single was certified gold.

"The Rose" as a 45 vinyl single has been available for many years in the Atlantic Oldies Series (ST-A-38228 SP) backed with Bette's cover of "When a Man Loves a Woman."

Critic Stephen Holden of the *Village Voice* wrote of *The Rose*:

"Quite simply, Bette Midler still doesn't know what to do with her voice. Since her Janis-like singer-on-the-skids character in *The Rose* didn't have to deliver great rock performances, only the ragged outlines of them, Midler carried off the part. But the soundtrack album makes clear just how far off the mark Midler fell vocally. However emotionally persuasive Midler's Joplin imitations may be, they're musically excruciating."

Divine Madness

ORIGINALLY RELEASED AS ATLANTIC #16022
NOVEMBER 3, 1980

(Atlantic Remastered Series CD #82781)

Produced by Dennis Kirk

Big Noise From Winnetka
Paradise
Shiver Me Timbers
Fire Down Below
Stay With Me
My Mother's Eyes
Chapel of Love/Boogie Woogie Bugle Boy
E Street Shuffle/Summer (The First Time)/Leader of the Pack
You Can't Always Get What You Want/I Shall Be Released

Highest position on *Billboard* Top 200: #34

"My Mother's Eyes" was released as a single on January 17, 1981. In *Billboard*, it reached #39. "My Mother's Eyes" was recorded during the concerts used for the filming of *Divine Madness*, but did not make the final cut due to time constraints. In addition to that song, "Shiver Me Timbers" and one other, "Rainbow Sleeve," do not appear in the home video versions of the film.

Once again, backup vocals were provided by Luther Vandross and Ula Hedwig, among others.

Bette dedicated this album to the film's executive producer, Howard Jeffrey. Interestingly, in 1991, Barbra Streisand dedicated one of the discs—the seventies—from her four-CD *Just for the Record* retrospective boxed set to Howard Jeffrey, too.

Divine Madness *captured the*
Divine Miss M *in concert.*

No Frills

ORIGINALLY RELEASED AS ATLANTIC #80070

AUGUST 1, 1983

(Atlantic Remastered Series CD #82783-2)

Produced by Chuck Plotkin

Is It Love
Favorite Waste of Time
All I Need to Know
Only In Miami
Heart Over Head
Let Me Drive
My Eye on You
Beast of Burden
Soda and a Souvenir
Come Back Jimmy Dean

Highest position on *Billboard* Top 200: #60

Three singles were released from *No Frills.* "Beast of Burden"—with an accompanying video featuring Bette and Mick Jagger—reached #71 on the *Billboard* chart. "All I Need to Know" made it to #77, and "Favorite Waste of Time" climbed up to #78, according to *Billboard.*

"Soda and a Souvenir" has Katey Sagal, Ula Hedwig, and Linda Hart backing Bette, labeled as "the Staggering Harlettes."

Bette cowrote "Come Back Jimmy Dean" with Jerry Blatt and Brock Walsh.

Bette offered special thanks to Benoit V. Gautier, her boyfriend at the time.

"Favorite Waste of Time" was the only song of Bette's her future husband, Martin von Haselberg, had ever been familiar with when they met!

In the January 31, 1986, *USA Weekend,* Bette recalled the making of *No Frills,* and found it wanting: "The last record I made, I was in the studio for over a year, and I don't like that process. There's so much technology, whatever humanity I had was slowly being eroded. And I spent a year making that record and nobody bought it. Nobody cared about it except me."

Mud Will Be Flung Tonight!

ATLANTIC #81291-2

NOVEMBER 1985

Produced by Bette Midler, Bob Kaminsky, and Jerry Blatt
Written by Bette Midler

Additional material by Jerry Blatt, Frank Mula,
Lenny Ripps, Marc Shaiman,
Charlene Seeger, and Bruce Vilanch
Music arranged and played by Marc Shaiman
Recorded at Budd Friedman's Improvisation
(in Los Angeles),
April 30–May 1, 1985

Taking Aim

Fit or Fat: "Fat as I Am"

Marriage, Movies, Madonna, and Mick

Vicki Eydie: "I'm Singing Broadway"

Coping

The Unfettered Boob

"Otto Titsling"

Why Bother?

Soph

When this album was released, it included a label that read: "This album contains material that may be deemed offensive by Bruce Springsteen, Madonna, and Prince—For adults only." This was a parody of the then hot-button issue of music censorship and labels to warn of offensive lyrics.

A group of videos called *Bette's Bits* were created to help promote *Mud Will Be Flung Tonight!* They were staged and directed by Jerry Blatt, with Bonnie Bruckheimer producing. These bits included Bette as Soph, for the first and only time in costume; a musical segment for Vicki Eydie; the very world-weary woman wondering, "Why Bother?"; and Bette as Bette dishing about Madonna and "We Are the World," among other things. According to Bruckheimer, "We decided to go with a series of interchangeable 'bits' because we realize that music video programmers don't really like comedy videos, and if we went with one three-minute clip, it probably wouldn't get shown."

Beaches

(Original Soundtrack Recording)

ORIGINALLY RELEASED AS ATLANTIC #81933
NOVEMBER 22, 1988

Produced by Arif Mardin

Under the Boardwalk
Wind Beneath My Wings
I've Still Got My Health
I Think It's Going to Rain Today
Otto Titsling
I Know You by Heart
The Glory of Love
Baby Mine
Oh Industry
The Friendship Theme

Highest position on *Billboard* Top 200: #2
Status: Triple Platinum

A single of "Wind Beneath My Wings" was released on April 15, 1989. It was on the *Billboard* chart for fifteen weeks and became a #1 single—the only one Bette has ever achieved (so far). It was a certified gold record (sales of one million units) and won Grammys for Best Record and Best Song.

After the success of "Wind Beneath My Wings," a second single from the film was released, "Under the Boardwalk," backed with film composer Georges Delerue's "The Friendship Theme" (Atlantic #7-88976). "Boardwalk" failed to make it onto the *Billboard* chart.

The cassette version of *Beaches* features a different mix of "Under the Boardwalk" and a completely different vocal on "Baby Mine."

Bette cowrote "Oh Industry."

When interviewed in October 1990 by the *New York Times,* Bette commented: "After I got beaten up on my third record, I wanted to be in the vanguard of what was going on. Everyone I knew was listening to disco music, and in my inimitable fashion, I leaped

on that bandwagon, but my foot slipped. I went on to make a couple of real clunkers. Instead of trusting my own instincts, I was trying to squeeze myself into this or that mold. I think that the *Beaches* material is close to what I should have been doing all along."

Scott Haller of *People* wrote of *Beaches:* "It's the powerful ballads that really proved Midler doesn't have to be coddling a dying friend on screen to move an audience. 'Wind Beneath My Wings' (previously recorded by such people as Sheena Easton, Willie Nelson, and Perry Como) articulates the movie's theme of enduring friendship, and Midler's heartfelt delivery conveys the message a lot more succinctly and satisfyingly than the film. As a movie, *Beaches* isn't exactly divine. As a soundtrack, it rates an *M* for marvelous."

Beaches *became the ultimate Bette album.*

Some People's Lives

ORIGINALLY RELEASED AS ATLANTIC #82129

SEPTEMBER 25, 1990

Produced by Arif Mardin
Associate producer: Marc Shaiman

One More Round
Some People's Lives
Miss Otis Regrets
Spring Can Really Hang You Up the Most
Night and Day
The Girl Is on to You
From a Distance
Moonlight Dancing
He Was Too Good to Me/Since You Stayed Here
All of a Sudden
The Gift of Love

Highest position on *Billboard* Top 200: #6
Status: Double Platinum

"From a Distance" was released as a single on October 20, 1990. It was on the *Billboard* chart for nineteen weeks, reaching as high as #2. But the popularity of the song was enduring. It became the unofficial theme for Operation Desert Storm, and was ultimately certified platinum. "Night and Day" was also released from *Some People's Lives;* it reached #62 on the *Billboard* Top 100 chart.

After the success of "From a Distance," the song "Moonlight Dancing" was released as a twelve-inch dance single in early 1991.

Former Harlettes Ula Hedwig and Charlotte Crossley provided background vocals. Cissy Houston and the New Hope Baptist Church of Newark, New Jersey, also sang behind Bette, specifically on "From a Distance."

In the *Chicago Tribune*, November 8, 1990, critic Jan DeKnock wrote: "Count on the divine—and maddeningly diverse—Miss Midler to come up with an album like this one. . . . It has been eight years since Midler released an album (other than soundtrack projects), so it isn't surprising that she would try to cover so much territory here. Although the kicky stuff is fun, the album's best tracks are its ballads, including the haunting title track and the current single, 'From a Distance.' "

For the Boys

(Music from the Motion Picture)

ORIGINALLY RELEASED AS ATLANTIC #82329

NOVEMBER 12, 1991

Produced by Arif Mardin
"The Girl Friend of the Whirling Dervish"
produced by Marc Shaiman
"In My Life" and "Billy-a-Dick" coproduced with Marc Shaiman
"Vickie and Mr. Valves" coproduced with Dave Grusin
"Every Road Leads Back to You" coproduced with Joe Mardin

Billy-a-Dick

Stuff Like That There

P.S. I Love You

The Girl Friend of the Whirling Dervish

I Remember You/Dixie's Dream (duet with James Caan)

Baby, It's Cold Outside (duet with James Caan)

Dreamland

Vickie and Mr. Valves

For All We Know

Come Rain or Come Shine

In My Life

I Remember You

Every Road Leads Back to You

Highest position on *Billboard* Top 200: #22

Status: Gold

"Every Road Leads Back to You" was the single release. It charted in *Billboard,* but only as high as #78.

"Billy-a-Dick" was an unpublished Hoagy Carmichael song, which pianist Michael Feinstein brought to Bette's attention.

Melissa Manchester, a former Harlette, and Patty D'Arcy had small roles in the film and sang with Bette on "Billy-a-Dick."

"Baby, It's Cold Outside" was shot as a scene in the film, but wound up being used over the end credits as only a vocal. The movie included an instrumental version of "For All We Know," while the album has Bette's vocal.

Stephanie Zacharek in *Entertainment Weekly* reviewed the *For the Boys* soundtrack, writing: "Her reading of Hoagy Carmichael's 'Billy-a-Dick' is set off nicely by caramel-cream harmonies reminiscent of the

"Stuff Like That There" was a dynamic number from **For the Boys.**

Andrews Sisters; she gets that end-of-shore-leave feel on the pensive "For All We Know"; and on 'Stuff Like That There,' her bravura leaves even a tight horn section in the dust. But *For the Boys* also includes newer songs. . . . Midler really spoils the fun when she soars—all the while on automatic pilot—through the record's closer, the sterile soft-rock ballad 'Every Road Leads Back to You.' It's a shame Midler opens the record standing so tall, only to fall off her platform shoes with a thud."

Experience the Divine:
Bette Midler's Greatest Hits

ORIGINALLY RELEASED AS ATLANTIC #82497

JUNE 1993

Compiled and produced by Arif Mardin
and Bette Midler

Hello in There

Do You Want To Dance?

From a Distance

Chapel of Love

Only in Miami

When a Man Loves a Woman

The Rose

Miss Otis Regrets

Shiver Me Timbers

Wind Beneath My Wings

Boogie Woogie Bugle Boy

One for My Baby (And One More for the Road)

Friends

In My Life

Highest position on *Billboard* Top 200: #50

Status: Gold

"One for My Baby (And One More for the
Road)" was not previously on any Bette Midler
album. It was taken from Bette's Emmy-winning
appearance on *The Tonight Show Starring Johnny
Carson* on May 21, 1992.

Performing songs from **Gypsy** *at the 46th Emmy
Awards (UPI/Corbis-Bettman)*

Gypsy

(Original Soundtrack Recording)

Originally released as Atlantic #82551

November 9, 1993

Soundtrack produced by Arif Mardin, Michael Rafter,
and Curt Sobel
Coproduced by Robert Shaper Jr.

Overture

May We Entertain You

Some People

Small World

Baby June and Her Newsboys

Mr. Goldstone

Little Lamb

You'll Never Get Away From Me

Dainty June and Her Farmboys

If Momma Was Married

All I Need Is the Girl

Everything's Coming Up Roses

Together, Wherever We Go

You Gotta Get a Gimmick

Let Me Entertain You

Rose's Turn

End Credits

Highest position on *Billboard* Top 200: #183

The *Chicago Tribune* music critic offered a glowing review: "The new version . . . is a class act, and this recording is another instance of what went right. Bette Midler, in the role she was born to play, showed gumption by performing a lot of the material live, during the actual filming. This studio version is altogether different, and even better. Silky studio magic has now been added to Midler's incomparable versions of such Jule Styne–Stephen Sondheim treats as 'Rose's Turn,' 'Small World,' and 'Some People.' Meanwhile, the slight harshness of timbre in 'Everything's Coming Up Roses' is now smoothed away. Television reviewers dubbed the telecast the performance of Midler's career; this is easily one of the finest of her albums—tough, brassy, but full of those satiny moments that so complement her persona."

In order to do the *Gypsy* score justice, Bette began studying voice with a new teacher, Marge Ringston. "[She] took my voice out of my throat and put it in my head. She helped me get a new set of vocal abilities that allowed me to choose songs I would never sing before, because I couldn't hit the notes without screeching. I'm not going to say I'm Maria Callas or anything, but I have made terrific strides. I'm not going to stop until I'm a great singer," Bette told Stephen Holden in the *New York Times.*

Bette of Roses

ORIGINALLY RELEASED AS ATLANTIC #82823

JULY 11, 1995

Produced by Arif Mardin
Associate producer: Buzz Feiten

I Know This Town

In This Life

Bottomless

To Comfort You

To Deserve You

The Last Time

Bed of Roses

The Perfect Kiss

As Dreams Go By

It's Too Late

I Believe in You

Highest position on *Billboard* Top 200: #45
Status: Gold

The song "To Deserve You" was released both as a cassette single (#4-87127) and CD single with dance mixes (#85531-2). The cassette single only featured a bonus cut, not available on any album, entitled "Up! Up! Up!"

Ula Hedwig, former Harlette, provided backup vocals.

Bette did interviews about *Bette of Roses* and discussed how she had retrained her voice: "It's really vocal technique. It's getting ahold of the voice and not letting it run away with you. When I did *Gypsy,* I had to really start to work on the voice. A lot of the material in *Bette of Roses* required big octave jumps, which I couldn't do before *Gypsy* and which were real, arduous work. I really like the sound of [my voice] now and the fact that it's more flexible."

The critics were impressed with *Bette of Roses*. Howard Cohen of the *Miami Herald* wrote: "Bette Midler's first studio album in five years is one of the summer's pleasant surprises. . . . Here she offers melodic tunes such as 'I Know This Town,' a spry Western winner, and the smoldering ballad 'To Comfort You,' in which she adopts a sultry lower register as brushes softly stroke against drums amid teasing, bluesy guitar licks. Seldom has Midler been so willing to use her full vocal range. . . . *Bette of Roses* isn't perfect. Midler's good-natured vulgarity and delightful brassiness of olden days is missing . . . and there are too many ballads. But overall, this is the best Bette in some time."

Additional Music Notes

Bette recorded "It's Gonna Take a Miracle" with the Manhattan Transfer for their 1994 album, *Tonin'* (Atlantic #82661-2).

Bette provided vocals for two Disney animated features and was heard on the soundtrack albums: *Oliver & Company* (1988), "Perfect Isn't Easy"; and *The Hunchback of Notre Dame* (1996), "God Help the Outcasts." On the soundtrack album for *That Old Feeling*, Bette's vocal, "Somewhere Along the Way," was a highlight.

Bette wrote the song "Blueberry Pie" with Bruce Roberts and Carole Bayer Sager for a 1980 album entitled *In Harmony: A Sesame Street Record*. It won a Grammy Award and was also featured on the 1991 Disney AIDS charity album, *For Our Children*.

Bette contributed the song "Sweet and Low" to the album *Carnival! The Rainforest Foundation Tribute*. According to the liner notes, the song was one of her mother's favorites.

Bette recorded a song for the closing credits to *Stella*. Entitled "One More Cheer," it has never been released as a single or on any album. Her duet with Trini Alvarado of "California Dreaming" is also heard in the film, but has never been recorded for an album.

Bette recorded Cole Porter's "You Do Something to Me" for the closing credits to *Scenes From a Mall*. The recording has never appeared on any album.

Bette recorded "I Put a Spell on You" for both a sequence in, and the closing credits of, *Hocus Pocus*. A promotional CD of the score from that film was created; it was never sold in retail stores . . . and Bette's recording was not included on the promo.

After Bette of Roses, *Bette left Atlantic Records for Warner Bros.*

Although Rose was a self-destructive woman, Bette gave her great spirit and humor.

FIVE

The Films of Bette Midler

The Rose

TWENTIETH CENTURY-FOX, 1979

CREDITS:

Producers: Marvin Worth and Aaron Russo; Director: Mark Rydell;
Screenplay: Bill Kerby and Bo Goldman; Cinematographer: Vilmos
Zsigmond; Film Editor: Robert L. Wolfe; Music and Music
Arrangements: Paul A. Rothchild; Art Direction: Jim Schoppe;
Costume Design: Theoni V. Aldredge; Choreography: Toni Basil
MPAA Rating: R; Running Time: 134 minutes

CAST:

Bette Midler as Rose; Alan Bates as Rudge Campbell; Frederic
Forrest as Houston Dire; Harry Dean Stanton as Billy Ray; Barry
Primus as Dennis; David Keith as Mal; Sandra McCabe as Sarah

SYNOPSIS

Rose is a rock singer whose life is out of control. She is a brilliant star
who is overwhelmed by the demands of her career and desperately in
need of time off. Her manager, Rudge, refuses her request, and Rose
turns to booze, drugs, and sex for solace. Rose thinks she has found
the man of her dreams when she hooks up with Houston, an AWOL
soldier, but he cannot put up with the craziness of her lifestyle. When
Houston leaves her on the brink of her hometown concert in Miami,

Rose is devastated. She does heroin, liquor, and pills, then manages to give her last performance before dropping dead on stage.

REVIEWS

"This movie about the pressures of rock stardom and its road tours is told from the inside in two ways: Midler and the filmmakers know what it's like because they've been there, and the movie also concentrates on staying mostly inside the Rose character's head. The Rose handles its locations and supporting characters in that way, from Rose's point of view, so that cast members swim in and out of focus and we're seduced into Rose's state of mind. That makes the movie's gradual descent from good times to disquiet, pity, doom, and silence an especially effective one."
—Roger Ebert, *Chicago Sun-Times*

"What a storm of acting! Midler loads her own brassy, elbow-swinging, big-mama sluttishness on top of Janis's childlike egocentricity, and the results are emotionally kaleidoscopic, draining, yet clear as a series of trumpet blasts."
—David Denby, *New York*

The Rose was the role that made Bette Midler a movie star.

Bette Midler's success in *The Rose* should have spelled the beginning of a great film career. However, for a time it seemed that *The Rose* would be an isolated instance for Midler, making her a one-shot wonder. Fortunately, that was not the case. Bette Midler was destined to be a major film star, and though she faltered along the way, *The Rose* was the beginning of a long and accomplished body of work for Bette.

The Rose was a project that had been contemplated for years.

Based loosely on the career of Janis Joplin, a script called *The Pearl* had been offered to Bette soon after Joplin's death. She turned it down at that time in part out of respect for Joplin's memory, but when the project came back her way a few years later as *The Rose,* Bette reconsidered. Her renewed interest was due to the fact that it was no longer a Joplin biography, although Rose was a character clearly patterned after Janis. Bette understood the world Rose inhabited, and that character's symbiotic, albeit destructive, relationship with Rudge was more than a little reminiscent of Bette's troubled alliance with Aaron Russo. And whatever doubts Bette had about re-creating Joplin's magic on stage, she was confident that she would dig down deep enough and find the stuff to make Rose come alive on screen. "*The Rose* was a violent picture. Not violent with guns, but violent in language and emotion . . . just the kind of movie I wanted to do," Bette explained.

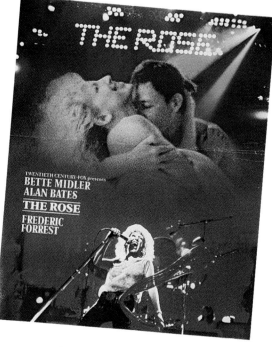

Her confidence was well founded. Bette Midler's performance in *The Rose* is nothing short of spectacular. She is completely alive and truthful, the essence of the twisted, tortured, and terribly talented Rose, a woman trapped by her success and yearning for the love and simplicity of an idealized childhood. And Bette did not bend the role to suit her own very famous stage persona. Rose was not the Divine Miss M in any way, shape, or form. If anything, fans going to *The Rose* expecting to see Miss M might have been disappointed. Guided by director Mark Rydell, Midler brought the randy, sassy, sad Rose to life, imbuing her with dimension and making her anguish all too real. It wasn't a pretty picture, but it was always great screen acting.

Bette was aided by a superb supporting cast. British theater and film star Alan Bates was an odd choice for Rudge, Rose's dominating, manipulative, and complicated manager. But in many ways his teddy-bear gruffness and slangy British accent supplied the exotic touch needed for *The Rose,* and he provided a great contrast to Frederic Forrest's down-to-earth, good old boy Houston Dire. Forrest's performance—understated and unassuming—was so good it was nominated for a Supporting Actor Oscar. One other performance was also integral, even though it was very small: Sandra

The Rose was a critical and commercial success world-wide.

McCabe as Rose's former lesbian lover. The scene between McCabe and Midler was remarkably frank and seemed very, very real. When asked about it when the film was released, Bette revealed, "That was a nightmare. I'm real straight, but we were really trying to be sympathetic. I jumped into it, hugging and kissing this girl." The point of the scene was much more than titillation. It illustrated Rose's desperate need for love, as well as her bisexual nature. And within the rock 'n' roll milieu, it was the essence of verisimilitude. Reportedly, Aaron Russo was furious with Bette for that scene. He felt it was *too* realistic.

Critics were united in their adoration of Midler; she was rewarded with the kind of reviews Barbra Streisand received for *Funny Girl* and Audrey Hepburn got for *Roman Holiday*. However, unlike Streisand and Hepburn, Bette didn't win the Oscar her first time out. She was nominated, but—unfortunately—she lost to Sally Field *(Norma Rae)*. Years later, Bette would complain that she had been robbed, and in retrospect, she probably was. Although Field's performance was wonderful, she did win again for *Places of the Heart*, and Bette has to date never had another role as riveting and compelling as Rose.

The Rose stands out among all Midler films for its realistic, deglamorized depiction of the music world. And while it did incorporate some aspects of Bette's own story—the chase scene through a Turkish bath, the musical number with drag queens—it was essentially a tragic tale of a self-destructive and needy human being. Bette more than lived up to Joplin's legend, and it's her performance that distinguishes *The Rose* from all other rock 'n' roll dramas.

When Houston deserts her, Rose cries out in agony.

Divine Madness

WARNER BROS., 1980

CREDITS:
Producer: Michael Ritchie; Director: Michael Ritchie; Executive Producer: Howard Jeffrey; Screenplay: Jerry Blatt, Bette Midler, and Bruce Vilanch; Cinematographer: William A. Fraker; Film Editor: Glenn Farr; Music—Music Arrangement and Supervision: Tony Berg and Randy Kerber; Production Design: Albert Brenner; Costume Design: Robert DeMora; Choreography: Toni Basil; Background Vocals: Luther Vandross
MPAA Rating: R; Running Time: 91 minutes

CAST:
The Divine Miss M: Bette Midler; Head Usher: Irving Sudrow; the Harlettes: Jocelyn Brown, Ula Hedwig, and Diva Gray; Band Vocals: Tony Berg, Jon Bonine, Joey Carbone, and Randy Kerber

SYNOPSIS

This film documents a concert by Bette Midler given at the California Civic Auditorium in Pasadena, California.

REVIEWS

"We need to see Bette Midler's body in movement. When she tries to be still and make it just on her singing, her act dies. It's not that she's a bad singer but that her voice alone isn't very distinctive—it lacks personality. The joy she communicates is in the feeling she gives you that she needs to move and bounce and take those quick trotting steps— just as she needs to sing and grin and tell dirty jokes."

—PAULINE KAEL, *NEW YORKER*

Bette was trim and sexy in this skintight outfit. (Warner Bros.)

"Bette Midler is a wonderful performer with a high and infectious energy level and a split-second timing instinct that allows her to play with raunchy material instead of getting mired in it. She sings well, but she performs even better than she sings: she's giving a dramatic performance in music, and Divine Madness *does a good job of communicating that performance without obscuring it in the distractions of most concert documentaries."*

—ROGER EBERT, *CHICAGO SUN-TIMES*

Divine Madness *advertising promoted Bette as a national institution.*

*D*ivine Madness is a time capsule version of Bette Midler on stage—up to 1980. "This show is the end of what I've been doing for five years on the stage. . . . It's a performance, it's a character that has developed over the years," Bette told Roger Ebert. The goal was clear: take Bette's *Divine Madness* tour and put it on film. That was director Michael Ritchie's task, but capturing the greatness of Bette Midler live in the spotlight is as elusive as trying to catch lightning in a bottle. Ritchie gives it his best shot, but *Divine Madness* can only approximate what Bette is like live. Still, as a concert film, *Divine Madness* works very well.

Ironically, the filming of *Divine Madness* was far from smooth. In 1983, Bette told *Village Voice* columnist Arthur Bell some of the problems: "Director Michael Ritchie hates music. Who knew? I didn't find out until the movie was edited that he not only dislikes music, he can't count a bar. Here was this tall cold man directing a diminutive waif from the streets of Honolulu. Oh, my dear. I really had to grin and bear that one. The Ladd Company came to me with Michael Ritchie under their arms. Well, I'll tell you, Alan Ladd Jr. had just started his movie company and thought *Divine Madness* would be a divine way to make money—not an epic or anything, just a small picture with a big star. Immediately, the project became nervewracking. I had a band that would tear their clothes off because they didn't like their costumes. I had a choreographer who screamed at the designer. The man who did my lighting and Michael Ritchie despised each other. In the middle of all this, I came down with pneumonia."

And then there was the weather. Torrential rains had soaked Pasadena and flooded the basement of the Civic Center where they filmed. There were even concerns about electrocution because of the lights and cameras needed and the water that was all over the place. Bette's pneumonia was also very serious. She was running a fever of 103 degrees. She would have liked to cancel the filming for another time, but that was simply not possible. Therefore, being a trouper, she did her best, and the filming commenced. To this day, though, she does not recall the experience of making *Divine Madness* with any joy.

In fact, she loathes watching it because it brings back nothing but bad memories.

For fans, *Divine Madness* achieves its goal. It is a wonderful look back at Bette, the way she was at that time and in that place. The repertoire includes songs from *The Rose*—"The Rose" to "Stay With Me"—as well as material from her earlier successes: "I Shall Be Released," "Leader of the Pack," and "Do You Want to Dance?" Delores DeLago is on display, and there are Soph jokes aplenty. Seventeen years later, *Divine Madness* holds up as prime Midler—a best Bette—even if it's only an approximation of the magic she makes in concert live!

You would never know how sick Bette was when **Divine Madness** *was filmed. (Warner Bros.)*

Jinxed

METRO-GOLDWYN-MAYER/UNITED ARTISTS, 1982

CREDITS:
Producer: Herb Jaffe; Director: Don Siegel; Cinematographer:
Vilmos Zsigmond; Film Editor: Doug Steward; Screenplay: Bert
Blessing and David Newman; Art Direction: Ted Haworth; Music
Score: Miles Goodman and Bruce Roberts
MPAA Rating: R; Running Time: 103 minutes

CAST:
Bette Midler as Bonita; Ken Wahl as Willie; Rip Torn as Harold;
Val Avery as Milt; Jack Elam as Otto; Benson Fong as Dr. Wing

SYNOPSIS

Once upon a time there was a gambler named Harold who had a jinx on a blackjack dealer named Willie. Wherever Willie goes, Harold shows up and wins at his table, forcing the casino to fire Willie. The only way for Willie to break the jinx is to take something from Harold, something like his girlfriend, Bonita, a lounge singer. Bonita is unhappy with Harold, who is cruel and abusive to her. She falls in love with Willie and the two conspire to kill Harold to cash in on his life insurance policy. Before they can pull off the murder, Willie defeats Harold and breaks the jinx. He decides to run off with Bonita rather than kill Harold. However, they find that Harold has committed suicide. Impulsively, they decide to use Harold's dead body to fake an automobile accident and then collect on the policy. When they discover that the policy has lapsed, they break up. Bonita tracks down the mysterious treasure Harold has left her, which turns out to be the secret of Harold's jinx on Willie. She shows up at his blackjack table and wins big. Later on, she shares the wealth with Willie, and they reunite.

REVIEWS

"Midler is not overly concerned with building a plausible characterization. Her performance is more on the order of creative sabotage, injecting sassy Midlerian one-liners to pep up a discombobulated storyline. There's no way of knowing what this bizarrely patchy movie started out to be—a love story? A comic Double Indemnity*? . . . Director Don Siegel is hardly known for comedy. On* Jinxed *he may not have known that he was making one until he saw the rushes."*

—DAVID ANSEN, *NEWSWEEK*

"Watching Jinxed *is like playing craps with loaded dice—there's no way you can win. Every scene comes up snake eyes. . . . The story has comic possibilities but it's so poorly directed, acted and produced that the title must have seemed prophetic to everyone involved. The big problem, and I do mean big, is Midler. The Divine Miss M, who delivered an outstanding impersonation of Janis Joplin in* The Rose, *seems to be doing an impression of a bleached blonde hyena on a bad trip. She bellows, screams, yells, chatters, blathers, shrieks, squeals and howls her way through her role as a small-time country singer. She steals so many scenes that the Screen Actors Guild should put out an APB. In fact, the only scenes worth watching feature Rip Torn trying to give her a dose of her own medicine by picking his nose."*

—MICHAEL BLOWEN,
BOSTON GLOBE

Everything you need to know about Bette's third film, *Jinxed,* is in the title. Never before had she been connected to a project that was so beset with problems and cursed upon execution. Bette takes full responsibility for bad judgment. She was without Aaron Russo, flying solo for the first time in years, and she jumped at the chance to do another picture. "*[The Rose]* did good business, I got fabulous reviews, I was nominated for an Oscar. But the fact is I never got another offer. I died. I was devastated. I really felt I had been shut out." That was Bette's state of mind, and it clearly clouded her reason-

Bonita was a lounge singer,
not unlike Vicki Eydie.
(MGM/UA)

ing. *Jinxed* seemed a good prospect—a comedy—and she grabbed it. If she had looked before she leaped, Bette might have thought better of this project and the director she allowed to guide her.

Director Don Siegel was clearly the wrong choice for *Jinxed*. An action director who had specialized in Clint Eastwood pictures *(Coogan's Bluff, Two Mules for Sister Sara, The Beguiled, Dirty Harry)*, Siegel had no affinity for comedy. It's anybody's guess why Siegel wanted to direct a Bette Midler movie, and make no mistake, this was a Midler movie. On the heels of *The Rose*, she was the main draw. Ken Wahl was a hunky young actor who had been in *Fort Apache, the Bronx,* but he was hardly a star, and Rip Torn was only a supporting player. Bearing that in mind, you would think that *Jinxed* would have been geared to bring out the very best of Bette, tailored to her talents, and that she would have been surrounded with a production team who knew that. It never happened. If anything, Siegel was intent on undermining Midler, Wahl disliked her on sight, and the project became more of an action-comedy than a Bette Midler vehicle. By the time the shoot was finished, Siegel (and Wahl) were bad-mouthing Bette all over Hollywood. Right or wrong, she became the fall guy for *Jinxed* —the reason for the picture's failure.

The experience of *Jinxed* was abysmal for Bette, and she suffered because of it. She didn't work in movies for four years. Interestingly enough, Bette's instincts were not entirely off. Comedy is her forte, and *Jinxed* might have been an amusing caper—a kind of romp like *How to Steal a Million*—with a better director at the helm and a stronger, more simpatico leading man. But the script for *Jinxed* simply wasn't funny enough, and Siegel's direction was far too heavy-handed. There are scenes that are beyond the realm of even black humor—for example, Bonita's encounter with the old prospector, Otto. There's a cruelty and brutality directed to Bette in that sequence that makes it almost painful to watch. Was that Siegel's true feelings coming through? Bette told *People* in 1983 that during the

*Everything about **Jinxed** was jinxed for Bette Midler.*

shoot, Siegel even raised a hand to her. "He hauled off and hit me."

The other aspect of the film that had a chance of working was the romance, but there was no chemistry between Bette and Ken Wahl. As Bette proved in *The Rose*, she can be a very compelling romantic leading lady. However, whatever bad feelings she and Ken Wahl shared, they were evident on screen. According to Wahl, he disliked Bette intensely. "It was miserable working with her, and it took all my concentration to get up and go to work in the morning," he told *People*.

Without any romantic or sexual tension, Bonita and Willie's love affair is unconvincing. By contrast, in *The Rose*, you felt Rose's anguish when she lost Dire, and you believed the passion in their love scenes. *Jinxed* didn't have a second of that kind of emotion in the love story.

All in all, *Jinxed* was Bette's greatest misstep. Though not totally her fault, she endured the defeat and walked away wiser for the experience. "I was in a very vulnerable position then because I had left Aaron [Russo], who had looked after me for seven years. So I threw myself into a project that I never should have gotten mixed up with. *Jinxed* was a traumatic experience, but I don't think it was that bad a picture. He [director Don Siegel] actually cut it quite sensitively. Even though he didn't like me, he didn't make me look bad."

Jinxed was a dismal failure at the box office, which was just as well for Bette. The fewer fans who saw *Jinxed*, the better. In 1987, after getting her film career back on track, Bette told Gene Siskel, "I had it pretty tough after *Jinxed*. I was professionally shattered. I had no personal involvement with anyone. I went on tour, got sick, canceled dates and tried to redo them. It was not a good time." Fortunately, good times were not too far down the road for Midler—just a few years.

A black cat is a bad luck omen, and it was for Bette in **Jinxed.** *(MGM/UA)*

Down and Out in Beverly Hills

Buena Vista, 1986

CREDITS:
Producer: Paul Mazursky; Director: Paul Mazursky;
Screenplay: Paul Mazursky, Leon Capetanos, and René Fauchois;
Cinematographer: Donald McAlpine; Film Editor: Richard Halsey;
Production Design: Pato Guzman; Art Direction: Todd Hallowell;
Costume Design: Albert Wolsky; Music: Andy Summers;
Song by the Talking Heads: "Once in a Lifetime"
MPAA Rating: R; Running Time: 103 minutes

CAST:
Nick Nolte as Jerry Baskin; Richard Dreyfuss as Dave Whiteman;
Bette Midler as Barbara Whiteman; Little Richard as Orvis
Goodnight; Tracy Nelson as Jenny Whiteman;
Elizabeth Peña as Carmen; Evan Richards as Max Whiteman;
Mike as Matisse the dog

SYNOPSIS

A depressed, homeless man named Jerry Baskin decides that life is not
worth living when his dog runs away from him. Determined to kill
himself, he jumps into the Beverly Hills swimming pool of the
Whiteman family. Dave Whiteman saves Jerry and invites him to
rebuild his life by staying in their poolhouse. Barbara Whiteman is
appalled at first, but slowly, Jerry ingratiates himself with the entire
family. He ends up helping each member of the clan to solve many of
their problems, but in doing so, he threatens Dave's position as family
leader. Jerry decides to leave, but Dave, Barbara, and the family all
realize that they don't really want him to go and ask him to stay. Jerry
turns them down until he realizes that he cares about them, too—too
much to go.

REVIEWS

"Welcome, once again, to Jean Renoir's Boudu Saved From
Drowning *(1932), which Paul Mazursky has revised, possibly with
half an eye on* My Man Godfrey *. . . Mazurky varies Renoir's ending.
. . . Indeed, the old film that* Down and Out *most consistently evokes
is Mazurky's own* Bob & Carol & Ted & Alice. *. . . Well, Disney did
produce the film, and on the basically farcical level where it chooses to
stay, it is a funny and likable movie."*

—RICHARD SCHICKEL, *TIME*

"Poor Barbara complains of not having had an orgasm in nine and a half years; by casting Bette Midler in the role, Mazursky makes this sound like the film's only understatement. Even when these good folks and their guests end a party by jumping fully clothed into the swimming pool, we are given to understand that this is not merely funny (which, incidentally, it isn't), but also touching; a need to experience, to feel, to live. Mazurky's people are not acutely, not cutely, crazy, like that adorably snarling and amusingly biting pooch Matisse, and all it will take to cure them is a lovable and loving derelict. Jerry promptly displays remarkable

sanity, astuteness, and therapeutic skills. . . . What the unthinking Mazursky intended as a sappy, sentimental ending turns out to be the nearest the film gets to satire: It is heartlessly amoral for anyone not too brainless to think it through."

—JOHN SIMON, NATIONAL REVIEW

*D*own and Out in Beverly Hills is the film that is credited with beginning the run of box office successes that turned the Disney Studios film division into an industry powerhouse. It is also the picture that supposedly "saved" the careers of Bette Midler, Richard Dreyfuss, and Nick Nolte. In many ways, it's both. *Down and Out* was the first film under the Jeffrey Katzenberg–Frank Wells–Michael Eisner administration, the first R-rated adult comedy for Disney, and the film that rediscovered the considerable talents of Midler, Dreyfuss, and Nolte. The trio had all been in career slumps: Bette's due to *Jinxed* and her inactivity because of

Aside from Bette Midler and Richard Dreyfuss, Little Richard also added star power to **Down and Out in Beverly Hills.**

that failure; Dreyfuss and Nolte because of bad career choices complicated by substance abuse problems. In Hollywood circles, Disney was taking a big chance hiring these three, even though they had all been successful, bankable stars just a few years before. There was some sense that one, both, or all of them would break under the strain of a new production and sink Disney's investment. In retrospect, this seems a ridiculous notion, but that was the atmosphere at the time. And when Paul Mazurky guided Midler, Dreyfuss, and Nolte to a smash comedy hit, Disney publicity reinforced the notion by gloating about how risky *Down and Out in Beverly Hills* really was.

One of the strengths of **Down and Out** *was the chemistry between Bette and Richard Dreyfuss.*

In hindsight, everything seemed stacked in Disney's favor. The combination of Midler, Dreyfuss, and Nolte was dynamite, especially when these pros were given the kind of quality satire Mazurky and cowriter Leon Capetanos created for them. Based on the French film

Boudu Saved From Drowning by Jean Renoir, *Down and Out* skewered Los Angeles and the nouveau riche 1980s. The mate-rial was ripe for the picking, and Mazurky rose to the occasion, as did his stars. Filming was easy, and everyone worked well together. After the trou-bles on *Jinxed* and *Divine Madness,* Bette was thrilled with the jovial Paul Mazursky. "I thought I was going to meet some silver-haired Hollywood type, but Paul turned out to be an ex–stand-up comic, a guy with whom I had instant rapport. He runs a very cheerful set, jolly, in fact, to the point of mania. And that's the way to make a pic-ture," she told Thomas O'Connor in the *New York Times.*

There were no unfortunate incidents or problems. Bette even suggested that the stars' problematic past added something indefin-able to the process. She told Gene Siskel, "Paul Mazursky, our direc-tor, used to call Richard Dreyfuss and Nick Nolte and me 'the Betty Ford gang.' We all had our problems, and I think that was part of why he cast us and part of the unwritten appeal of the movie."

Down and Out was one of the most successful comedies of 1986—earning $60 million—and reopened doors all over Hollywood for Bette. From her point of view, she was back, and she had every intention of staying.

Ruthless People

BUENA VISTA, 1986

CREDITS:
Producer: Michael Peyser; Directors: Jim Abrahams, David Zucker, and Jerry Zucker; Screenplay: Dale Launer; Cinematographer: Jan DeBont; Film Editors: Arthur Schmidt and Gib Jaffe; Music: Michel Colombier; Art Direction: Donald Woodruff; Costume Design: Rosanna Norton
MPAA Rating: R; Running Time: 93 minutes

CAST:
Danny DeVito as Sam Stone; Bette Midler as Barbara Stone; Judge Reinhold as Ken Kessler; Helen Slater as Sandy Kessler; Anita Morris as Carol; Bill Pullman as Earl

SYNOPSIS

Clothes manufacturer Sam Stone arranges to have his obnoxious wife, Barbara, killed. Before the hit takes place, though, Ken and Sandy Kessler kidnap her. They are out to get even with Sam, who has stolen

Sandy's idea for a Spandex miniskirt and made a fortune. They try to get Sam to pay them back by ransoming Barbara, but Sam refuses to pay. He figures this is the best way to get rid of his wife. Complicating matters are Sam's mistress, Carol, and her idiot boyfriend, Earl. In the end, Barbara bonds with Sandy and Ken, and they conspire to swindle Sam and give him a taste of his own medicine.

REVIEWS

Kidnapped by K Mart or Donald Duck? (Touchstone)

"Ruthless People *is the kind of Hollywood comedy you can never get enough of, in the summertime or anytime. It's light, fast, funny, and not too nice. You don't need to know more about the plot complications, except perhaps that Midler loses weight with unforeseen consequences. Her outrage when she learns that DeVito won't even ransom her for a bargain-basement $50,000 is cherishable. The actors, including Bill Pullman, as Morris's dumb peroxide-blond stud, all look good, especially Midler. The down-and-dirty* Ruthless People *is the comedy that for the first time this year entitles Hollywood to dust off the word 'romp,' after a year of supposed comedies that suggest a fleet of cement mixers struggling up a hill in low gear.*"

—JAY CARR, *BOSTON GLOBE*

"Directed by the trio of cutups who brought us Airplane! *and* Top Secret!*—Jim Abrahams and David and Jerry Zucker—*Ruthless People *is that rarest of screen commodities: a knockabout farce that's so cleverly constructed and scripted that its escalating coincidences and jumped conclusions (over an X-rated videotape) seem almost plausible . . . Midler, who was very pregnant at certain stages of production,*

plays on every woman's mania for the perfect size-six bod. Her kicking, scratching, intimidating 'victim' puts the afternoons of casual confinement to good use: She sweats off every last ounce of flab, until the transformation from braying fatso to svelte superstar is complete. Midler's turn from kidnapee to member of the kidnap gang when she learns she's been marked down is funnier than anything the actress does in Down and Out in Beverly Hills. *Her crude prescription for revenge will have you squealing and squirming all at once."*
—GLENN LOVELL, SAN JOSE MERCURY NEWS

O n the heels of *Down and Out,* Bette was Disney's fair-haired girl. The studio was anxious to use her comic talent, and as *Ruthless People* neared production—and Madonna passed on the key role of Barbara Stone—

Locked up, Barbara decides to exercise and lose weight.
(Touchstone)

Bette was ready, willing, and able to do the part.

Ruthless People was loosely based on the O. Henry short story "The Ransom of Red Chief," about a group of kidnappers who snatch an obnoxious child and then pay the parents to take the brat back. Screenwriter Dale Launer, however, claimed that he got the idea from the Patty Hearst kidnapping. In the role of Sam Stone's obnoxious wife, Bette had the kind of over-the-top, broad and brassy character she could sink her teeth into. Directors Jim Abrahams and the Zuckers soon learned they had made the right choice: Bette was a far more capable and inventive comedienne than Madonna.

On screen, Sam Stone hated his wife Barbara. Off screen, Danny DeVito and Bette Midler became instant friends.

Bette was unafraid to play Barbara Stone in the broadest strokes, to make her loud and vulgar and nasty. She didn't hedge her bets or worry about how she looked: she gave herself to the part, and it's that kind of courage that makes her such a good actress. There is no funnier moment on screen in *Ruthless People* than when she learns that her husband has refused the kidnappers' demands—which have been reduced time and again. As she learns that she's been marked down, Bette's face tells the story and punctuates the joke. As she whimpers, "I've been kidnapped by K Mart," the moment is brilliantly realized, and Bette hits the mark perfectly. Nobody could have done the scene better.

Bette was making a name for herself at Disney, becoming the most important woman on the lot since Minnie Mouse. Disney signed her up for four more films and encouraged her to begin developing her own projects. Bette's fortunes had changed indeed.

Outrageous Fortune

TOUCHSTONE, 1987

CREDITS:
Producers: Ted Field, Robert W.
Cort; Director: Arthur Hiller;
Screenplay: Leslie Dixon;
Cinematographer: David M.
Walsh; Music: Alan Silvestri;
Costume Design: Gloria
Gresham; Film Editor: Tom Rolf;
Production Design: James D.
Vance
MPAA Rating: R; Running Time:
99 minutes

CAST:
Shelley Long as Lauren Ames;
Bette Midler as Sandy Brozinsky;
Peter Coyote as Michael Santers;
Robert Prosky as Stanislav; John
Shuck as Atkins; George Carlin as
Frank; Anthony Heald as Weldon

SYNOPSIS

In acting class, straight-laced Lauren clashes with her polar opposite, the street-wise Sandy. Lauren and Sandy are both sleeping with the same guy, Michael Santers, a fact that they don't discover until he is killed in an explosion. At the morgue, when Lauren and Sandy find that he faked his death, they agree to team up to try to find him. Along the way, they learn Michael is an ex–CIA agent who has stolen a rare chemical virus and threatens to use it unless the government pays him $20 million. The mismatched duo become friends as they are threatened and nearly killed tracking Michael down. In the end, Lauren and Sandy get back at Michael, save the country by finding the virus, and even manage to do *Hamlet* on Broadway, with Lauren as Hamlet and Sandy as Ophelia!

REVIEWS

"There are a lot of terrific things in Outrageous Fortune, *a flawed but often hilarious new comedy, and two of the most terrific are Midler*

Shelley Long and Bette Midler had great chemistry in **Outrageous Fortune.** *(Touchstone)* *and Long, a comedy team that might well become the female sex's answer to Laurel and Hardy or Crosby and Hope."*

—John H. Richardson, *Los Angeles Daily News*

"Femmeraderie—the complementary palship of two women—has buttressed many a TV sitcom, from I Love Lucy *to* Laverne and Shirley *to* Kate and Allie. *But partnering in Hollywood action comedy is usually considered guy stuff. So with a simple twist of gender, screenwriter Leslie Dixon can give the most arthritic situations a fresh and frisky bounce. She can also fashion smart dialogue, cut to character. Bullying her way onto an airplane headed west, Sandy bluffs, 'There's a kidney in Kansas City that ain't gettin' any fresher.' Each time, Sandy brazens the pair in and out of scrapes; Lauren leaps over impossible obstacles. Together they make one dynamite heroine. They also make* Outrageous Fortune *the best movie about under-employed actors wearing drag to save their skins since* Tootsie.*"*

—Richard Corliss, *Time*

Chemistry is an elusive commodity in film, especially in comedy. Either actors have it or they don't. *Outrageous Fortune* has great chemistry. The unlikely pairing of Shelley Long and Bette Midler, plus a lively script by Leslie Dixon, is nothing short of magical. Like Lucy Ricardo and Ethel Mertz, Long and Midler sparked each other. Their inspired lunacy makes *Outrageous Fortune* a joy.

The idea for the picture was hardly original. Men had been doing action-buddy comedies for years—*Butch Cassidy and the Sundance Kid, 48 Hours,* et al.—with great success to boot. But women as partners on screen was rarely—if ever—proposed. The thought was that women couldn't get along; they could only compete. This was ludicrous, of course, as *Outrageous Fortune* proved. For *Outrageous Fortune,* Shelley Long—fresh from her hit TV series *Cheers*—was teamed with Bette, Disney's hot new comedy queen. They are both very funny ladies, but would they work together as buddies on screen? Wisely, they were chosen not for their similarities but for their differences. Where Long is uptight, Midler is free and easy. Where Long is finicky and haughty, Midler is loose and vulgar. They're an *Odd Couple* coupling, and the oil-and-water combination was a great mix. Added to the mix was the notion that their characters were in love with the same man; thus they were competitors. But as the story unfolded and it became clear that the guy was a heel who had wronged both women, the girls bonded. They were both scorned, and together they displayed a furiously funny fury.

Director Arthur Hiller was on familiar turf with *Outrageous Fortune.* Elements in the story were very much like *Silver Streak*—the CIA, the chase, the unlikely teaming of two funny performers (Gene Wilder and Richard Pryor). Like *Silver Streak, Outrageous Fortune* was a crowd pleaser. The film was the third in Bette's Disney trilogy of comedy successes, following *Down and Out in Beverly Hills* and *Ruthless People.*

While shooting the picture, Bette was under a lot of stress. Not only did she learn that she was pregnant, but her father, Fred, died. "But she never missed a call, never even missed a line," her costar Peter Coyote recalled. The physical nature of the film was a hardship, and Bette had stunt doubles, but many shots were all Bette. In fact, in the scene where she and Long try to stop a truck on a deserted highway, Bette improvised a fall in front of the oncoming ten-wheeler. Ever the professional, she did what she thought was funny for the scene, and the fall was a fake, a theatrical stunt, which didn't hurt the baby one bit. As for Bette's relationship with the reportedly difficult Shelley Long, the ladies got through the picture without incident. Just in case, Disney made sure the billing, the number of lines, and even the dressing rooms were equal.

In 1991, long after *Outrageous Fortune* was released and a hit, Bette revealed how she felt about working with Long: "I didn't really get along very well with her. I was pregnant at the time. It was very hot, I was fainting, it was just unpleasant. She lets a lot of things get in her way. But I can't fault her performance, she's a wonderful actress." Too bad, because a reteaming of Long and Midler could still be box office gold again, not to mention a very funny film. After all, Newman and Redford gave it another go, and look how well *The Sting* turned out.

Frank lends Sandy his mule to get away from the bad guys. (Laurel Moore/Touchstone)

Oliver & Company

WALT DISNEY, 1988

CREDITS:
Director: George Scribner; Screenplay: Jim Cox, Timothy J. Disney,
and James Mangold; Music: J.A.C. Redford; Supervising Animators:
Mike Gabriel, Glen Keane, Ruben A. Aquino, Hendel Butoy, Mark
Henn, and Doug Krohn
MPAA Rating: G; Running Time: 72 minutes

CAST:
Bette Midler as Georgette; Joey Lawrence as Oliver; Billy Joel as
Dodger; Cheech Marin as Tito; Richard Mulligan as Einstein;
Roscoe Lee Browne as Francis; Sheryl Lee Ralph as Rita

SYNOPSIS

Oliver & Company is a cartoon modernization of Charles Dickens's classic *Oliver Twist*. Oliver, a little lost kitten, becomes part of a group of stray dogs, including Dodger. The dogs work for their master, Fagin, robbing people. While on a job with Dodger, a little girl named Jenny finds Oliver and takes him home with her. Jenny has a beautiful show dog named Georgette, who is instantly threatened by Oliver. When Fagin discovers that Oliver has landed in a rich home, he steals Oliver back—with Georgette's help—and holds him for ransom. In the end, Dodger and his friends rescue Oliver, making sure he is happily reunited with Jenny.

REVIEWS

"The prima donna moxie in Bette Midler's voice makes this poodle a pistol. Descending a staircase to a nifty Barry Manilow tune called 'Perfect Isn't Easy,' she's a Joan Crawford–bitch on four legs and a diamond leash. [Oliver & Company] *is too slight to rank with such Disney groundbreakers as* Pinocchio *and* Fantasia; *the film is more on the good-fun level of* The Lady and the Tramp *and* 101 Dalmatians. *But why kick? With its captivating characters, sprightly songs and zap-happy animation,* Oliver & Company *adds up to a tip-top frolic."*

—PETER TRAVERS, *PEOPLE*

"Oliver & Company [is] the first animated feature from the new Disney studio regime, which is promising one such picture each year.

Their first effort, measured against the Disney legacy of classics, is not up to the highest standard. Even though it's based on Oliver Twist, *it's more of a modernization of* Lady and the Tramp, *and modern in this case means a jumble of voices and moods. That narrative is interrupted too often with songs: Dodger sings about 'street savoir-faire' and a prissy French poodle screeches about pulling herself together each morning. The musical voices belong to Billy Joel and Bette Midler, respectively, but this material is far afield of their best work. As a result, a Chihuahua (voice by Cheech Marin) steals the movie with wisecracks."*

—GENE SISKEL, *CHICAGO TRIBUNE*

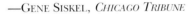

As part of Bette's extended contract with Disney, she agreed to do a few ancillary projects for the studio. One of those projects was providing the voice for an animated feature. Over a couple of years—in "drips and drabs," as Bette recalled—Bette provided the vocals for Georgette, a haughty, purebred French poodle. In a sequence that showed off the latest in computer animation technology, Georgette sings "Perfect Isn't Easy," while descending a grand staircase.

Although given the prime Disney marketing treatment—commercials, toys, fast food tie-ins—*Oliver & Company* was not a big hit. Compared to the other Disney cartoon features of that era—*The Little Mermaid, Beauty and the Beast,* and *Aladdin* — *Oliver & Company* is a tepid effort. Although the occasional use of dazzling computer techniques that were perfected in just a few years with *Beauty and the Beast* helped, most of *Oliver & Company* is simplistically drawn. The level isn't much higher than Saturday morning cartoon fare and that hurt the film overall.

Still, thanks to the Disney cachet, *Oliver & Company* did decent business on its initial release, as well as on its re-release in 1996. As for Bette personally, she could show the feature to her daughter, Sophie, with a sense of pride in being part of the grand Disney tradition.

As part of her Disney deal, Bette provided the voice for Georgette in **Oliver & Company**.

Big Business

TOUCHSTONE, 1988

CREDITS:

Producers: Steve Tisch and Michael Peyser; Director: Jim
Abrahams; Screenplay: Dori Pierson and Marc Rubel;
Cinematographer: Dean Cundey; Film Editor: Harry Keramidas;
Production Design: William Sandell; Set Decoration: Richard C.
Goddard; Costume Design: Michael Kaplan; Music Direction: Marc
Shaiman; Music: Lee Holdridge
MPAA Rating: PG; Running Time: 93 minutes

CAST:

Bette Midler as Sadie Shelton/Sadie Ratliff; Lily Tomlin as Rose
Shelton/Rose Ratliff; Fred Ward as Roone Dimmick; Michele
Placido as Fabio Alberici; Barry Primus as Michael; Michael Gross
as Dr. Jay Marshall; John Vickery as the Hotel Manager

SYNOPSIS

*At a power breakfast at the
Plaza, Sadie Shelton has no
patience for her naive sister,
Rose. (Laurel Moore/
Touchstone)*

Two sets of identical twins—Sadie and Rose Ratliff and Rose and Sadie
Shelton—are mixed up at the time of their birth by a faulty-sighted
nurse. The mismatched sisters go on to wildly different lives, with the
country girl Sadie Shelton feeling as out of place in her life as the city
girl Rose Ratliff. When Moramax, the corporation run by the Ratliffs,

tries to close down a factory in Jupiter Hollow, the hometown of the Sheltons, Rose Shelton heads to New York to stop them, bringing Sadie with her. At the Plaza Hotel, the twins converge, and after a series of near misses, the sisters discover each other, save Jupiter Hollow, and each find the right man.

REVIEWS

"On paper, Big Business *looks unbeatable. Two Bette Midlers and two Lily Tomlins, playing mismatched sets of twins, accidentally separated at birth, meeting years later after a lot of mistaken identity stuff, one set rich, the other poor. You'd think it'd be four times as funny as the everyday Hollywood comedy, and twice as marketable. But there's something awfully earthbound and fabricated about* Big Business*. . . . Midler is all gusts and eruptions, a little orange-haired hurricane bopping through whatever landscape she occupies, oblivious to her surroundings, powered by heartfelt snorting. Tomlin is a comic guerrilla, sneaking up on her terrain and her characters, observing both sharply, then, when she's ready and comfortable, stringing together her brilliantly observed detail into full-fledged comic invention. The difference between Midler and Tomlin is the difference between persona and characterization. They never seem fully comfortable with one another here. That's the main reason the comedy in* Big Business *doesn't stride across the screen purposefully and confidently, the reason it so often seems to hang there, dangling uneasily and tentatively. At best,* Big Business *is fair to middling business."*

—JAY CARR, *BOSTON GLOBE*

In the film's special effects climax, the twins meet each other. (Laurel Moore/ Touchstone)

"Midler rescues scenes by using her clothes as props: when Sadie the mogul of Moramax flips up her collar, the gesture bespeaks perfect self-satisfaction. (Chaplin did this sort of thing, and he didn't do it better.)

And her snooty asides are terrific: this gorgon keeps her best lines to herself. This film often looks third class, and the plot keeps conking out, but its climax—when the two sets of twins finally confront each other—is a visual brain-twister. And Midler is a classic figure—a grinning urchin out of Volpone. *Her appetite is the audience's appetite. It's as if she and we were passing a flask of euphoria back and forth. More!"*

—PAULINE KAEL, *NEW YORKER*

Big Business has double Bette and double Lily, yet it's half as funny as it should be. The adventures of two mismatched sets of identical twins goes all the way back to Shakespeare's *A Comedy of Errors*. In *Big Business*, the twist on the old tale is the addition of modern technol-ogy. Using computers and split-screen techniques, direc-tor Jim Abrahams was able to stage Bette facing Bette in a variation of the classic mirror gag (see the Marx Brothers in *Duck Soup* or Lucille Ball and Harpo Marx in *I Love Lucy*), the difference here being that Bette was doing the scene with herself, not someone dressed and made up like her. The wizardry is dazzling, and it makes the climax of the film a knockout. The failure of the farce that came before it is what makes *Big Business* pleasant, but forgettable, entertainment.

Clearly, Disney was trying to recapture the magic of *Outrageous Fortune*, but unlike Long and Midler, Tomlin and Midler didn't really have good chemistry. Their scenes never click, in part because the material is not nearly as funny as you know Tomlin and Midler are in real life, as you've seen them in other projects. And they don't spark each other to create any kind of synergy. In 1991, Bette acknowl-

Despite their great comic talents, Bette and Lily Tomlin didn't really click as sisters in **Big Business.**

edged that she and Lily were at odds professionally. She told *Movieline's* Lawrence Grobel, "Well, Lily is really a perfectionist. I kept saying, 'Lily, this is the Midler School of Mugging, you just have to mug your way through this. Lil, it's very light, look, I'm singing with a cow! How deadly can it be?' But she just wouldn't buy it. I couldn't talk her into it. She really struggled with that material, she was so determined to get her message across. Her heart was in the right place, she wanted to make it better. But sometimes people don't have any patience for better, they just want to get it done. That picture typifies that, believe it or not."

As with *Outrageous Fortune, Big Business* had to deal with billing and keeping things equitable between Bette and Lily. They cleverly solved the problem of who got top billing by having the movie advertisements read "Bette Midler and Lily Tomlin and Lily Tomlin and Bette Midler in *Big Business*." Ultimately, *Big Business* did respectable—not big—business at the box office.

Beaches
BUENA VISTA, 1989

CREDITS:
Producers: Bonnie Bruckheimer-Martell, Bette Midler, and Margaret Jennings South; Director: Garry Marshall; Screenplay: Mary Agnes Donoghue, from a novel by Iris Rainer Dart; Cinematographer: Dante Spinotti; Film Editor: Richard Halsey; Production Design: Albert Brenner; Art Direction: Frank Richwood; Set Decoration: Garrett Lewis; Costume Design: Robert DeMora; Music: Georges Delerue
MPAA Rating: PG-13; Running Time: 110 minutes

CAST:
Bette Midler as C.C. Bloom; Barbara Hershey as Hillary Whitney Essex; John Heard as John Pierce; Spalding Gray as Dr. Richard Milstein; Lainie Kazan as Leona Bloom; James Read as Michael Essex; Grace Johnston as Victoria Essex; Mayim Bialik as C.C. (age 11); Marcie Leeds as Hillary (age 11)

SYNOPSIS

C.C. Bloom, the quintessential child performer, meets Hillary Whitney, a spoiled rich kid, on the beach at Atlantic City. Although they are from entirely different worlds, they form a friendship, which is strengthened over the years through letters. In their twenties,

Whitney and C.C. become roommates in New York City, and as their careers thrive—C.C. as an actress-singer, Whitney as a lawyer—their interest in the same man causes a strain in their relationship. Hillary moves to San Francisco and gets married. C.C. marries her director and becomes a big hit on Broadway. Both their marriages fail, and when Whitney has a child, it is C.C. who is by her side. Ultimately, when Whitney learns she is dying, she turns to C.C. to help her face death and to raise her daughter after she is gone.

REVIEWS

"Although we're only two weeks into 1989, we've already got a movie so resoundingly awful that it's bound to stand the test of time and emerge as one of the year's worst. Beaches *it's called—possibly because of the oceans of tears it means to jerk from the idea of a vicissitude-laden thirty-year friendship between a pair of never-the-twain-shall-meet women played by Bette Midler and Barbara Hershey, possibly because it's as involving as a dead whale. Midler, in effect, plays Midler, a pushy Bronx yenta who slugs her way to a big-time singing career. Hershey is the one you won't recognize. With her new surgically full lips and severely straight hair, she's a rich San Franciscan who has everything, including a law degree, yet gets nothing. They meet as eleven-year-old girls on one beach, at Atlantic City. Their story ends thirty years later on another, this one on the Pacific. . . . The reason the film never works is that we never get any of the girl talk that would have given the friendship (and the film) the kind of texture it needs to make it believable. . . . Every scene, every exchange, seems painfully calculated, telegraphed, plastic, especially the scene in which they finally air their respective jealousies. Heavy-handed, maudlin, bloated and tin-eared,* Beaches *is the kind of camp classic that could set female bonding back fifty years."*

—JAY CARR, *BOSTON GLOBE*

*"*Beaches *[is] a much too mechanical tearjerker about the tears and laugh-filled friendship between an earthy singer and an uptight rich woman. Bette Midler and Barbara Hershey star as the friends, brought together as children in the film's best scenes and, later, as women competing for the same man and as friends pushed to the limit by personal and professional problems. I heard some sniffling among some audience members, but the story goes for one situation that is guaranteed to produce sympathy. Aside from*

Mayim Bialik (**right**) *as the young C.C. was perfectly cast.* (Touchstone)

for one n that is guaranteed to produce symnpathy. Aside from that, we never accept Midler in her relationship with John Heard. Only her occasional singing redeems an otherwise emotional roller coaster that travels in slow motion. Barbara Hershey is wasted in a boring role."

—GENE SISKEL, *CHICAGO TRIBUNE*

Iris Rainer Dart wrote *Beaches* with Bette Midler in mind. C.C. Bloom was a role that was made for Bette Midler; so much so, that many people think C.C. was Bette—and vice versa. Bette acknowledged that C.C. was nearly a perfect fit: "This character wasn't really hard at all. I had lived a lot of it. But I wasn't the out-and-out model for the character. Other people are in there—Cher, for one, so I've heard, but I'm not sure which parts."

Whether C.C. was totally Bette or not, the audiences didn't care. They loved her, and they loved the story of friendship between women over the years. *Beaches* was the kind of crowd pleaser that defies the critics. Everything about the movie was sentimental and corny and old-fashioned, but filmgoers—especially women—embraced it. They did so despite the uniformly horrendous reviews doled out by the press. After the fact, Bette reflected on the situation, saying, "*Beaches* touched a huge chord in women, but it was reduced to

tearjerker status by fifty-year-old male reviewers who feel they've been manipulated when they start to cry."

Fortunately for Bette, *Beaches* was critic-proof. It did very respectably at the box office, and the music she sang in the film was widely accepted. One song—"Wind Beneath My Wings"—was destined to be a hit, even though Bette was not shown singing it in the movie. Director Garry Marshall and coproducer Bonnie Bruckheimer-Martell felt that Bette's performance was so powerful that it would have taken the audience "out" of the movie, reminding viewers that she was Bette Midler, not C.C. Bloom. Therefore, "Wind" was heard over a film montage. Ultimately, it didn't matter. The soundtrack album became the biggest recording success of Bette's career, and the single of "Wind Beneath My Wings" was her first—

Director Garry Marshall had great rapport with his stars. (Louis Goldman/Touchstone)

C.C. meets John when she delivers a singing telegram to him dressed as a bunny

and only—number one hit. The single went on to win Grammys for Best Record and Best Song. (Because "Wind Beneath My Wings" was not originally composed for the film, it was not eligible for an Oscar nomination.)

One of the strengths of *Beaches* was the casting. Aside from Bette, Barbara Hershey was an inspired choice for Hillary Whitney. As with Shelley Long (in *Outrageous Fortune*), Bette had great chemistry with her costar. Another brilliant stroke was the casting of Mayim Bialik as the young C.C. Bialik was a pint-sized version of Midler, complete with the big voice, comic timing, and the suggestion of deep vulnerability. After the success of *Beaches*, Bialik went on to have a long-running NBC sitcom success as the title character in the

Despite their differences, Hillary and C.C. became life-long pals.

114

sitcom *Blossom*. Lainie Kazan as C.C.'s stage mother was also excellent casting. The only detriment casting-wise was the generally weak actors chosen as the weak men in Hillary and C.C.'s lives.

Beaches was not completely faithful to Dart's novel—a bestseller—but it was close enough. The strength of the story was the friendship between two very different ladies—Hillary Whitney and C.C. Bloom—and the way they grow over the years and in the face of tragedy. Bette thrived on the drama of the piece: "It's much deeper than anything I've done since *The Rose*. I like the fact the movie has sentiment, that people laugh one minute and cry the next. People don't get to do that at the movies too often, and I think that's one of the things that's magical about the cinema—indeed, all forms of theatrical endeavor. When you pay your money, you're paying to be carried away, to be transfixed, to be transported." *Beaches* more than succeeded. It swept audiences away and kept Disney smiling all the way to the bank.

Stella

TOUCHSTONE AND THE SAMUEL GOLDWYN COMPANY, 1990

CREDITS:
Producer: Samuel Goldwyn Jr.; Director: John Erman;
Screenplay: Robert Getchell, based on the novel by Olive
Higgins Prouty; Cinematographer: Billy Williams; Film
Editor: Jerrold L. Ludwig; Production Design: James Hulsey;
Art Direction: Jeffrey Ginn; Set Decoration: Steve
Shewchuk; Special Effects: Doug Graham and Martin
Malivoire; Makeup: Bob Mills, Suzanne Benoit, and Richard
Blair; Costume Design: Theadora Van Runkle;
Choreography: Pat Birch; Music: John Morris
MPAA Rating: PG-13; Running Time: 114 minutes

CAST:
Bette Midler as Stella Claire; John Goodman as Ed Munn;
Trini Alvarado as Jenny Claire; Stephen Collins as Stephen
Dallas; Marsha Mason as Janice Morrison; Eileen Brennan
as Mrs. Wil-kerson; Linda Hart as Debbie Whitman;
Ben Stiller as Jim Uptegrove; William McNamara as Pat
Robbins; John Bell as Bob Morrison;
Ashley Peldon as Toddler Jenny

SYNOPSIS

In 1968, Watertown barmaid Stella Claire meets a good-looking young
doctor named Stephen Dallas. Although she resists at first because
they are from such different worlds, she finally gives in and goes out
with him. Soon, they have an affair. When Stella becomes pregnant,
she refuses to marry Stephen or have an abortion. She raises her
daughter—Jenny—on her own without taking anything from Stephen.
Eventually, Stephen returns to be a real father to Jenny, showing her
the better things in life. Stella cannot compete—a fact reinforced
when she takes teenaged Jenny to a Florida resort and embarrasses her
daughter by her lack of social grace. Jenny turns resentful, but will not
turn on her mother. Stella realizes she has to push Jenny away and stay
out of her life so she'll have everything Stella never could give her. On
the day of Jenny's wedding to a society heir, Stella watches from a distance, content that she did right by her child.

REVIEWS

"Bette Midler stars in a laughably bad remake of Stella Dallas, *the
story of a working-class mother who sacrificed her own future for that
of her daughter. Stephen Collins is wildly miscast as the man who loves
Midler, and Trini Alvarado is too contemporary for the dated character
of the daughter. Nothing—absolutely nothing—works here in this
shoddy soap opera."*

Stella and her reason for

living, her daughter, Jenny

(Pat Harbron/Touchstone)

—GENE SISKEL, *CHICAGO TRIBUNE*

"Come back, Bette Midler. She is a true original. Why does she spend her time copying others? Especially since she's not doing it very well. She made her reputation, outside singing, as a rude, anticonventional comedienne. But her last film, Beaches, and her latest, Stella, are mainline tearjerkers. Not only that, the women she portrays basically contravene the various freedoms her comic work implied. In Stella, a remake of that weary weepy Stella Dallas, she tries to scoop up a little comedy as she floats down a stream of tears, but it's no use. Once she was very close to being a Brechtian epic actor. In fact, she once announced plans for a film on the life of Lotte Lenya. Where is it? Where is anything other than her two latest films? They're not only dreadful in themselves, they debase her talent. 'Tragedy tomorrow, comedy tonight,' sang Zero Mostel in A Funny Thing Happened on the Way to the Forum. Formerly divine Miss M, please heed."

—STANLEY KAUFFMANN, *NEW REPUBLIC*

Because it was her name above the title, Bette Midler took the rap for this third film version of Olive Higgins Prouty's famous novel *Stella Dallas*, but the real culprit was Jeffrey Katzenberg. As the head of Disney's film division at that time, Katzenberg acquired the rights from the Samuel Goldwyn Company to remake the story, which reached its zenith in the 1937 version directed by King Vidor. In that film, Barbara Stanwyck played Stella and was Oscar-nominated for her performance. Katzenberg loved the Stanwyck movie and thought it could be a wonderful vehicle for Bette. For the 1990 version, the blatantly old-fashioned story was uncomfortably updated to the 1960s. That was the film's first and most crucial error. The story of Stella's sacrifice for her daughter, based on her daughter's embarrassment about her mother's low-class station in life, didn't play in modern times.

To play the ultimate good mother, Bette drew on her own mother for inspiration. (Pat Harbron/Touchstone)

Stella was actually schizophrenic about its updating. On one hand, Stella very frankly considers her choices when she becomes pregnant—having a legal abortion, marrying Stephen, or raising the child on her own. On the other hand, Stella is completely uneducated about the better things in life and doesn't assimilate anything from movies or television. The whole notion of "classes," being completely outmoded, hampered *Stella* from the start.

At the time of its release, Bette defended the film and gave the credit/blame for it to Katzenberg. "They told me to do it. Jeffrey [Katzenberg] had it in his mind to do it for a long time; he always loved it. He got a wonderful script, and Sam Goldwyn had the rights to it because it was his father's picture. Jeffrey paid buckets for it, so I read it, and it's a good script. I don't exactly do what they tell me without putting up a fight, but I really couldn't say no to this because he paid so much money for it. Actually, I couldn't watch the first version. I saw only half about twenty-five years ago. I said, 'Gee whiz, Jeffrey, it seemed pretty sentimental.' But I don't think the new version has to be that way." It didn't have to be, but it was.

Stella opened with little fanfare and was quickly thrashed by the critics. After the sentimentality of *Beaches*, Bette was accused of wallowing in another soap opera. But unlike *Beaches*, Stella didn't have a "Wind Beneath My Wings" to save it. It did miserably at the box office. Bette's take on the film's poor performance was that people simply didn't know about it. Whether that was the case or not, *Stella* did nothing good for Bette Midler's film career.

Stella *was a dream film for studio head Jeffrey Katzenberg.*

Scenes From a Mall

BUENA VISTA, 1991

Credits:

Producer: Paul Mazursky; Director: Paul Mazursky; Screenplay:
Roger L. Simon and Paul Mazursky; Cinematographer: Fred
Murphy; Film Editor: Stuart Pappe; Production Design: Pato
Guzman; Art Direction: Steven J. Jordan; Costume Design: Albert
Wolsky; Music: Marc Shaiman
MPAA Rating: R; Running Time: 87 minutes

CAST:

Bette Midler as Deborah Fifer; Woody Allen as Nick Fifer; Bill
Irwin as Mime; Paul Mazursky as Dr. Hans Clava

SYNOPSIS

On the day of their sixteenth wedding anniversary, Nick and Deborah
Fifer go shopping and plan their big party for that night. Nick is a
very successful sports lawyer, and Deborah is a psychologist and
author of a bestselling self-help book. On the surface, they have a
great marriage. However, as the day progresses, Nick confesses his
extramarital affairs to Deborah, and she tells him she's been cheating
on him with her psychiatrist. Despite their problems, Nick and
Deborah realize they still love each other and want to stay together.

REVIEWS

*"Both Allen and Midler are required to play the scenes realistically, but
as performers, they are inherently too stylized for such a trite, knowing,
'psychological' approach to marital weariness. Hampered, they don't do
as well as regular dramatic actors would have in the same roles.*
Scenes From a Mall *is not a dud—there are a few jokes—but it left
me with an almost mournful sense of disappointment."*

DAVID DENBY, *NEW YORK*

*"Put Woody Allen's urban angst together with Bette Midler's brash
earthiness and director Paul Mazursky's loud vulgarity and what do
you have? A mess. . . . This might have been hilariously heartrending,
but Mazurky and fellow scriptwriter Roger L. Simon have failed to
find the tone that would emulsify the oil that is Woody and the water
that is Bette. The result is two stars without a twinkle."*

GINA MALLET, *CHATELAINE*

Paul Mazurky's notion for *Scenes From a Mall* was an examination of modern marriage. Even the title was remotely similar to Ingmar Bergman's dramatic *Scenes From a Marriage.* As in *Down and Out in Beverly Hills,* Mazurky chose to satirize Southern California, setting the action in the Beverly Center shopping mall. Despite the setting, the story was essentially just a two-character piece. The machinations of the Fifer marriage were more tedious than hilarious, and with no other major characters to distract from the main duo, there was little relief to their on-again, off-again bickering and making up.

Woody Allen, in only his second acting role in a picture he did not write or direct himself, was an audacious choice for Nick. While there was nothing wrong with Allen's performance, there wasn't anything right about it either. And for one of the only times on screen, Allen was paired with a Jewish leading lady rather than a traditional WASP. According to Paul Mazursky: "We went over every name. But we decided we didn't want to cast the film as if it were a Woody Allen film. We wanted to put him with someone far away from the type he normally casts, you know, the goyishe [Gentile] fantasy, Mia Farrow or Diane Keaton. We wanted to marry him to someone he normally might cast as his sister. So we came up with Bette."

Unfortunately, Bette and Woody had no on-screen magic. Perhaps they were supposed to be comfortable with each other—like an old married couple—but on screen that didn't add up to an exciting love story. And again, as in Bette's teaming with Lily Tomlin, you just knew these two people were funnier than the material they were given to enact.

Scenes From a Mall had none of the wit of *Down and Out in Beverly Hills,* Bette's previous collaboration with Paul Mazursky. But even if Bette was disappointed that *Scenes* failed at the box office, she was thrilled to have had the experience of working with Woody Allen. "I hadn't had a crush like that since I married my husband. I love to scream and laugh and that's why I fell so in love with Woody. I would

Despite their best efforts, Bette and Woody couldn't make audiences laugh at their marriage in **Scenes From a Mall.** *(Brian Hamill/ Touchstone)*

laugh and laugh. I would pee! I would have to go and change my diaper. I swear to God."

In 1991, while promoting *For the Boys*, Bette recalled not only the experience of making *Scenes from a Mall*, but the disappointing results at the box office for it and *Stella:* "I was so slagged for *Stella*, I'm afraid to talk about it even to defend myself. *Stella* wasn't so bad. I guess people just read such terrible reviews that they decided they didn't want to spend their seven dollars. It wasn't that bad. I always cry when I look at it. I believe nobody saw that picture. And the same thing is true with *Scenes From a Mall.* I loved it. I loved making it, I loved being involved with Woody Allen and Paul Mazursky, and I sat in that screening room and I loved it. I was so shocked that people didn't go to see it. I was just dumbfounded. I said, 'Well, you know, you just throw up your hands. What do they want?' " Ultimately, Bette would get the answer when she made *The First Wives Club* in 1996.

For the Boys

TWENTIETH CENTURY-FOX, 1991

CREDITS:
Producers: Bette Midler, Bonnie Bruckheimer, Margaret Jennings South, and Mark Rydell; Director: Mark Rydell; Screenplay: Marshall Brickman, Neal Jimenez, and Lindy Laub; Cinematographer: Stephen Goldblatt; Film Editors: Jerry Greenberg and Jere Huggins; Art Direction: Dianne Wager and Don Woodruff; Set Decoration: Marvin March; Casting: Lynn Stalmaster; Costume Design: Wayne Finkelman; Choreography: Joe Layton; Music: Dave Grusin
MPAA Rating: R; Running Time: 145 minutes

CAST:
Bette Midler as Dixie Leonard; James Caan as Eddie Sparks; George Segal as Art Silver; Patrick O'Neal as Shephard; Christopher Rydell as Danny; Arye Gross as Jeff Brooks; Norman Fell as Sam Schiff; Rosemary Murphy as Luanna Trott; Dori Brenner as Loretta; Bud Yorkin as Phil; Jack Sheldon as Wally Fields; Shannon Wilcox as Margaret Sparks; Arliss Howard as Michael Leonard; Melissa Manchester as Corrine

SYNOPSIS

During World War II, Dixie Leonard, an aspiring singer, is given the chance of a lifetime when she's sent to work in a USO tour with the legendary comic Eddie Sparks. Dixie is a hit with the audience, but

Eddie initially resents her upstaging him. Eddie soon realizes that he and Dixie are a great team. They begin an uneasy partnership that lasts through the war and into the 1950s, when they have a hit TV show. Along the way, Dixie is widowed and Eddie becomes a surrogate father to her son, Danny. When Eddie betrays his head writer and Dixie's uncle, Art Silver, who is accused of being a Communist, the act breaks up. Years later, Eddie lures Dixie back to do a USO show in Vietnam, where Danny is stationed during the war. When the camp is attacked, Danny is killed. In 1991, for a TV special, Dixie agrees to appear one last time with Eddie. Alone before the show, she blames Eddie for Danny's death, but when they are united on stage, it's clear that some part of Dixie still loves Eddie.

REVIEWS

"In For the Boys, *Midler piles persona on top of persona on top of persona for two and a half hours in an attempt to overwhelm us with the sheer force and infinite variety of herself: She is the world. The movie, which was produced by her own company, has been constructed to serve as the Portable Bette—a boxed set of Midler moments, remixed and repackaged for Christmas giving. . . . In* For the Boys, *Bette Midler begins as a red-hot mama and winds up as Mother Courage. And the movie is such an ordeal that it turns into a demonstration of a startling theme: War is bad, but entertainment is hell."*

—PAULINE KAEL, *NEW YORKER*

"The movie is obvious in some ways and, I suppose, ripely sentimental, but it's also remarkably powerful and funny. It's easily the best movie about show business since The Rose, *which marked Midler's starring debut and the last time she worked with director Mark Rydell. . . . The final scenes, in which both Eddie and Dixie are so ancient they can barely move, are unusually honest about the bitter strength of egotism in old age.* For the Boys *is great entertainment, and it sees its gallant heroes so clearly that every emotion it squeezes out of us is fully earned and gratefully given."*

—DAVID DENBY, *NEW YORK*

Ultimately, **For the Boys** *failed at the box office.*

In many ways, *For the Boys* is the most ambitious and beloved project Bette Midler ever created. She conceived and nurtured it through years of development, realized it though production, promoted it in every media imaginable, and was ultimately heartbroken when the film failed to become the commercial success she hoped it would be. Still, *For the Boys* was a personal triumph for Bette, and it enhanced her reputation within the Hollywood community as much as her hot box office tenure with Disney had.

For the Boys reteamed Bette with director Mark Rydell for the first time since *The Rose*. Again, they were dealing with show business, but unlike the rock 'n' roll milieu of *The Rose, For the Boys* covered the changing world from the 1940s to the 1970s as reflected by two stars who entertain the troops in World War II, the Korean War, and Vietnam. It was also a story about a conflicted, complicated woman. As Bette commented, "I was interested in the story of a woman who raises a boy, and is crazy about him, but in the end sends him off to war. I knew the arena."

It was Rydell's idea to cast James Caan as Eddie Sparks, having worked with Caan in *Cinderella Liberty*. Bette was unsure about Rydell's choice, equating Caan with his tough guy image in pictures like *The Godfather*. It was only after viewing *Funny Lady*, the 1975 musical Caan did with Barbra Streisand, that Bette saw how capable Caan was at singing and doing comedy. Their collaboration was a good one, and Bette and Jimmy enjoyed working together. It was only after the film was released and fared poorly at the box office that Caan criticized Midler.

Preproduction for *For the Boys* was intense and complicated. Source music for the film had to be gathered, including period music for three different eras. For the forties sequence, when Dixie is first contacted to join Eddie, Bette wanted a song like "Boogie Woogie Bugle Boy." Pianist Michael Feinstein came up with just the song when he gave her a tape of Hoagy Carmichael's "Billy-a-Dick," which had been written in the forties, but never recorded. For a much later part in the film, when Dixie goes to Vietnam, Bette chose "In My Life," a Lennon-McCartney song she thought fit the situation perfectly.

Dixie sings "Come Rain or Come Shine" to her husband Michael.

To create the proper verisimilitude, Midler and Caan spent weeks learning to tap dance for the film. Another difficulty in pre-production was the complicated makeup and costume tests. Because the two characters had to age from their thirties to their eighties, costume, hair, and especially makeup tests were crucial. Once filming began, putting the old-age makeup on Bette, for instance, took four hours.

While scenes of the soldiers being entertained by Dixie and Eddie in World War II were being shot, reality asserted itself into the production when Operation Desert Storm was launched by President George Bush. The reserves who were playing extras in the picture were suddenly called into action, and as they prepared to be shipped overseas to the Persian Gulf, Bette and company found themselves living the story of *For the Boys*.

When the laser disc of *For the Boys* was released, director Mark Rydell provided a brief coda showing a few scenes from the film that had wound up on the cutting room floor because of the film's length. One was a gem for George Segal, a longer version of Uncle Art passing out Christmas gifts. Another was Eddie and Dixie's charming song-and-dance "Baby, It's Cold Outside," which was also done at the Christmas party. But the best of the bunch was a remarkably frank and romantic encounter between Michael and Dixie. It was to unfold after Dixie sings "Come Rain or Come Shine" to Michael, when the two are alone together. They are still dressed, but all entangled as they finish making love. The moment summarized the intensity of their love, the passion they shared, as well as depicting Michael's wildness—his desire to get closer to the combat zone—and Dixie's apprehension about his fate. Rydell apologized to actor Arliss Howard for dropping this crucial scene, but he also should have apologized to Bette. This scene would have done wonders to explain why her Dixie never loves another man again (although she does have a one-nighter with Eddie). Losing Michael is the key to her later bitterness. The love scene should have been retained.

Bette had high hopes for *For the Boys*. She felt it had everything that audiences loved about her—songs, dances, jokes, romance, drama. It was created as a vehicle to showcase the best of Bette. More than that, though, Bette really put her heart and soul into *For the Boys*. When the picture opened and a majority of critics gave it excellent notices, she was elated. But her happiness was short-lived. Within weeks of its opening, the picture slumped at the box office. Media mavens dubbed the movie a Thanksgiving turkey, and as new movies crowded the holiday season, *For the Boys* was shoved aside.

Winning a Golden Globe and an Oscar nomination for her performance as Dixie Leonard was of little comfort to her. In *Premiere* (August 1993), Bette was remarkably candid about how the *For the Boys* experience had hurt her: "I sulked and cried for so long after *For the Boys*, I didn't think anybody wanted to see me again. I turned down *Sister Act.* I turned down everything. I stayed home and planted a garden. . . . There's no logic to this business, and I was too naive to know it. Bottom line? *For the Boys* was my life. I developed it; I raised the money; I produced it. I killed myself making a picture for a grown-up audience, only to discover the grown-ups for whom it was made don't go to movies anymore. We took a poll, and one out of five kids didn't even believe World War II ever happened. We devised a brilliant marketing campaign for Fox, and Barry Diller rejected it, so nobody knew how to sell or promote it. *For the Boys* was doomed, and I took it personally. I gave them my heart, my guts, and my soul, and they didn't want it."

By 1995, Bette had had some time to reflect and was less bitter. She told Stephen Holden in the *New York Times:* "I had a big setback with *For the Boys*. Although I know privately what went wrong, I have no desire to point fingers. I was handsomely paid and did the best work I could, and people chose not to go to it. What can you do? You can't put a gun to people's heads and force them to go to your movie."

Dixie is reunited with her son, Danny, when she travels to Vietnam. (François Duhamel/20th Century Fox)

Hocus Pocus

Buena Vista, 1993

CREDITS:

Producers: David Kirschner and Steven Haft; Director: Kenny
Ortega; Screenplay: David Kirschner, Mick Garris, and Neil
Cuthbert; Cinematographer: Hiro Narita; Film Editor: Peter E.
Berger; Production Design: William Sandell; Art Direction: Nancy
Patton; Costume Design: Mary Vogt; Music: John Debney
MPAA Rating: PG; Running Time: 96 minutes

CAST:

Bette Midler as Winifred; Sara Jessica Parker as Sarah; Kathy
Najimy as Mary; Omri Katz as Max; Thora Birch as Dani; Vinessa
Shaw as Allison; Amanda Shepherd as Emily; Larry Bagby III as
Ernie ("Ice"); Stephanie Faracy as Jenny; Charlie Rocket as Dave

SYNOPSIS

*Bette received good notices,
but the movie didn't.*

In 1693, the three Sanderson sisters—Winifred, Sarah, and Mary—are
witches in Salem, Massachusetts. They are caught by the townspeople,
tried, and found guilty of sorcery. Before being hanged, they cast a
spell allowing them to come back to life in the future. In 1993, a

teenager named Max accidentally resurrects the three witches on Halloween. It falls to him, his sister, Dani, and his friend Allison to stop the witches who are trying to lure the children to their home and suck the youth from their bodies.

The Three Stooges? No, the Sanderson sisters in **Hocus Pocus.**

REVIEWS

"Hocus Pocus is a ninety-minute comedy without laughs. It is not funny, plain and simple. In other words, there is no magic to Hocus Pocus. *That* Hocus Pocus *is such a bore is through no fault of its stars; they simply do not have much of a script to work with. Midler and company do put their best face forward, which in this case is their ugliest face, as they mug their way through various situations. Only one remotely works, a rather spirited rendition of Screamin' Jay Hawkins's rhythm and blues classic, "I Put a Spell on You," but even Midler seems mildly embarrassed beneath all her makeup."*
—SHERMAN KAPLAN, WBBM NEWSRADIO 78, NEW YORK CITY

"Take three batty witches, a trio of photogenic children, one talking black cat, one slightly used blues song, and throw them all into a script. Now, say the magic words (Hocus Pocus) *and what have you got? Disney's half-baked recipe for box office success.* Hocus Pocus *is a*

pretty lackluster affair. . . . The wicked Sanderson sisters [are] a campy, quarrelsome lot, like Moe, Larry, and Curly in bordello drag. Despite the triple-threat actress combo, Hocus Pocus *won't be the* Sister Act *of 1993. There are a lot of gotta-sees this summer, and this isn't one of them."*

—JACKIE POTTS, MIAMI HERALD

Before it was released, Bette explained her reasons for doing *Hocus Pocus:* "I did [it] because I've got a six-year-old kid and there's nothing out there for her to see. It's harmless; it's got no four-letter words; the violence is minimal. It's broad and silly, but I don't have to worry about what I look like. . . . It's nice to just romp."

Somewhere between the drawing board and the execution, *Hocus Pocus* went poof. What emerged from the Disney Studios was not a wacky comedy about three ancient witches resurrected on Halloween to cause havoc in Salem, Massachusetts; instead, *Hocus Pocus* was an unfunny, unholy mess of a movie. Disney didn't even have their usually top-drawer marketing savvy on target for this film. They released it during the summer rather than Halloween, even though it was clearly a picture that would have benefited from the seasonal tie-in. But even a better release date wouldn't have helped *Hocus Pocus.* The problems with the film are inherent in the script.

As the three Sanderson witches—Winifred, Sarah, and Mary—Bette Midler, Sarah Jessica Parker, and Kathy Najimy are the best thing about *Hocus Pocus.* With better material, their comic antics and free-wheeling inanity might have been rollickingly funny. With better material, their bizarre anachronistic dilemma might have even been poignant. What might have been the three witches from *Macbeth* was reduced to lukewarm Three Stooges. Sadly, Bette is "Moe" in this triumvirate, a position that gives her nothing funny to do. Bette snarls and snaps; Parker is a cackling fool; and Najimy snickers and mugs. What's worse than their not being funny is that they're actually pretty scary. This is supposed to have been a children's film, yet the plot calls for the Sandersons to lure kids to their home to suck the life out of them! *Hocus Pocus* makes *Hansel and Gretel* seem benign.

Personally, Bette received some excellent notices for *Hocus Pocus.* She was complimented for giving Winifred a sinister—albeit comic—edge. Reflecting on the conundrum of doing well in a film that fails, Bette commented, "I think I do really good work, but it doesn't always wind up on the screen, so it's disappointing. I've been disappointed a lot, and I'm tired of being disappointed."

Apparently, she was disappointed enough to move on. For Bette, *Hocus Pocus* was the end of her magical run with Disney, an association that had helped put her into the top echelon of the film business and had been extremely beneficial for both the star and the studio. "I had a lot of fun at Disney for the first five pictures. But it got to a point where they wanted to do pictures with their own stamp and didn't want to hire outside writers. They wanted to have their own people, who worked for their prices, reporting to them. That's when things got dicey." Clearly, it was time to move on.

Gypsy

RHI ENTERTAINMENT, 1993

CREDITS:
Executive Producers: Robert Halmi Jr.,
Craig Zadan, Neil Meron, and Bonnie
Bruckheimer; Producers: Emilio
Ardolino and Cindy Gilmore; Director:
Emilio Ardolino; Book: Arthur Laurents;
Music: Jule Styne; Lyrics: Stephen
Sondheim; Choreography: Jerome
Robbins; Cinematographer: Ralf Bode;
Editor: William Reynolds; Production
Designer: Jackson Degovia
Not Rated; Running Time: 150 minutes

CAST:
Bette Midler as Rose; Cynthia Gibb as Louise; Peter Riegert as
Herbie; Ed Asner as Pop; Jennifer Beck as June; Lacey Chabert as
Baby June; Elizabeth Moss as Baby Louise

SYNOPSIS

The life story of burlesque queen Gypsy Rose Lee, from her childhood as an aspiring child star with a domineering stage mother named Rose. Rose attempts to push her daughters—June and Louise—onto the vaudeville stage, even as vaudeville is dying and movies are taking over

Bette in full force doing "Rose's Turn." (Tony Esparza/CBS)

Bette's performance as Rose in **Gypsy** *was dazzling.*

the theaters. She enlists the help of Herbie, a former agent, who helps Rose because he loves her. Slowly but surely, Rose alienates everyone in her life. They all leave her . . . except Louise, who becomes an unexpected success as a stripper—Gypsy Rose Lee, the Queen of Burlesque.

REVIEWS

*"*Gypsy *is a faithful adaptation of the 1959 stage hit that starred Ethel Merman, and it is vastly better than the 1962 film version with Rosalind Russell. Midler's skill and singing, which succeed in redefining and deepening the character, more than make up for the obviously flat and old-fashioned this-is-a-play-on-TV look of the film. The score, including such gems as 'Everything's Coming Up Roses' and 'You Gotta Have a Gimmick,' is extremely wide-ranging, and Midler scores knockouts with virtually every number. Supporting cast members, even Riegert, are surprisingly good singers, and Gibb, in a role that is more difficult than it appears, makes a star turn."*

—RICK KOGAN, *CHICAGO TRIBUNE*

"Botta-boom botta-Bette. To her many fans, the Divine Miss M has always been ridiculously sublime. And now, in the lustrous wake of her acclaimed concert tour of recent months, she adds to the mystique with a smashing network television movie debut in Gypsy. *This three-hour Midler tour de force—based on the famed Broadway musical—shimmers and soars with vintage show business pizzazz. If ever there was a harmonic convergence of star and role, it is here. Bette Midler was born to play Mama Rose, the ferociously obsessed stage mother at the bittersweet heart of* Gypsy.*"*

—MIKE DUFFY, *DETROIT FREE PRESS*

In the world of musical theater, *Gypsy* is one of the greatest shows ever created, and the role of Mama Rose is the quintessential star turn. For years, Bette Midler dreamed of playing Rose and singing the classic Jule Styne–Stephen Sondheim songs. "I never thought I'd be old enough to play this part. When you're very young, you imagine yourself with a lot of padding. As you grow older, you realize you don't need padding anymore." In 1993, Bette got the chance to fulfill her dream. After a successful new Broadway production, producers decided to commit *Gypsy* to film once more, only this time they would do it right. In 1962, when Warner Bros. brought the show to the screen, they altered the script, dropped songs, and miscast Rose with actress Rosalind Russell. For the new *Gypsy*, things would be different, starting with perhaps the very best musical performer in the world playing Rose—Bette Midler.

Once producers Robert Halmi Jr., Craig Zadan, Neil Meron, and Bonnie Bruckheimer had Midler, it was not too hard to convince the original creators—playwright Arthur Laurents, lyricist Sondheim, and composer Styne—to grant them the rights to redo *Gypsy*. They also promised to faithfully adapt the play, and committed to making *Gypsy* one of the most lavish TV productions ever. They had a $14 million budget and shot the film as if it were a feature. Director Emile Ardolino, who had directed *Sister Act, Dirty Dancing*, and the Oscar-winning short *He Makes Me Feel Like Dancing*, was chosen for his experience with musicals. Sadly, Ardolino was ill, and this was his last film. He died of complications from AIDS in November, just weeks before *Gypsy* had its broadcast premiere.

Bette was happy with the production. "It's as big as we could have made it. We treated it like a feature. We rehearsed for seven weeks before we even set foot on the soundstage." Producers even considered shooting the entire piece live—as if it were a real Broadway production. As Bette told reporters, "Mary Martin's *Peter Pan* was done on a soundstage and was completely live." Still, that was too risky a notion for CBS, but Ardolino and the producers did manage to have Midler and the others perform most of the show's big numbers live for the cameras rather than sing to a track and dub it after the fact. "It's live singing. That was a real step forward for us. That's hardly ever done anymore. It's a big challenge." Another innovation for *Gypsy* was shooting the film in long master scenes to simulate a Broadway play.

One of the highpoints of *Gypsy* is "Rose's Turn," the climactic number, which has been called the musical equivalent of a nervous breakdown. Every actress ever to play this role has had to rise to the occasion, and Bette was no different. "It's full of emotion, and it's very intricate. It has key changes and tempo changes. It's a terrifying piece of music because it's one of the two most famous arias in the musical comedy lexicon, the other one being the 'Soliloquy' from *Carousel.*" Bette's interpretation was one of the best things about *Gypsy,* a complete knockout.

Gypsy was broadcast on CBS-TV on December 12, 1993. It was hailed by the critics and did well in the Nielsen ratings. There was a lot of speculation about CBS producing other Broadway musical adaptations like *Gypsy,* including more with Bette. She mentioned titles like *Annie Get Your Gun, Mame,* and *Anything Goes,* in all of which she would be wonderful. Thus far, though, none of these shows has gone into production.

Get Shorty

MGM, 1995

CREDITS:
Producers: Danny DeVito, Michael Shamberg, and Stacey Sher; Director: Barry Sonnenfeld; Screenplay: Scott Frank, based on Elmore Leonard's novel; Cinematographer: Don Peterman; Editor: Jim Miller; Production Design: Peter Larkin; Music: John Lurie
MPAA Rating: R; Running Time: 105 minutes

CAST:
John Travolta as Chili Palmer; Gene Hackman as Harry Zimm; Rene Russo as Karen Flores; Danny De Vito as Martin Weir; Dennis Farina as Ray "Bones" Barboni; Delroy Lindo as Bo Catlett; Bette Midler as Doris

SYNOPSIS

Chili Palmer, a Miami collector for the mob, goes to Hollywood to track down a delinquent account and finds himself enmeshed in the movie business. Chili teams up with low-budget movie director Harry Zimm to get some thugs off Harry's tail and an "A" film off the ground.

REVIEWS

"Get Shorty is one of the sharper, funnier, better-cast, better-written movies around right now. But there's something about it that, well, comes up short. It's an intelligent, American studio comedy in an era where formulas are king, a not-too-guilty pleasure. . . . Though the inside jokes here—with unbilled actors like Harvey Keitel, Penny Marshall, and Bette Midler—are witty, somehow the machinations of Leonard's plot aren't engrossing enough to survive the absence of real tension. Leonard needs an undertone of danger for his offhand jokes and dialogue to work right."

—MICHAEL WILLINGTON, *CHICAGO TRIBUNE*

"Get Shorty finds a terrific ensemble cast going through the motions of a typical Elmore Leonard success story. . . . Get Shorty wouldn't be worth its mineral water without a self-deluding movie star, and it has one in the form of its title character, the very Dustin Hoffmanish Martin Weir. As skewered wickedly by Danny DeVito, Martin lives in a mansion replete with busts and portraits of himself and favors a restaurant table that lets him admire his latest billboard. . . . The full panoply of Hollywood types on parade here also includes Rene Russo, tough and winning as an actress whose specialty is screaming in horror films. There's also a quick cameo from Bette Midler as one very merry widow."

—JANET MASLIN, *THE NEW YORK TIMES*

This adaptation of Elmore Leonard's novel was the surprise comedy hit of 1995, and part of John Travolta's comeback, which began with *Pulp Fiction*. As a parody of Hollywood, *Get Shorty* was as smart and clever as Robert Altman's *The Player,* but with more good-natured humor. In a brief but integral extended cameo, Bette had one of her best comedy roles in years. It was such a brilliant turn that at the American Comedy Awards she was named Funniest Supporting Female even though she wasn't billed.

Get Shorty was produced by Danny De Vito, Bette's costar in *Ruthless People.* Bette had another reunion of sorts with Gene Hackman, with whom she played most of her scenes. Thirty years earlier, in *Hawaii*, Hackman had a supporting role, and Bette was a glorified extra, with no lines but more than one scene.

The First Wives Club

PARAMOUNT, 1996

CREDITS:

Producer: Scott Rudin; Director: Hugh Wilson;
Screenplay: Robert Harling, based on Olivia
Goldsmith's novel; Cinematographer: Donald
Thorin; Film Editor: John Bloom; Production
Design: Peter Larkin; Music: Marc Shaiman
MPAA Rating: PG; Running Time: 95 minutes

CAST:

Bette Midler as Brenda Morelli Cushman; Goldie
Hawn as Elise Elliot Atchison; Diane Keaton as
Annie McDuggan Paradise; Stephen Collins as
Aaron Paradise; Maggie Smith as Gunilla
Goldberg; Sarah Jessica Parker as Shelly; Dan
Hedaya as Morty Cushman; James Naughton as
Gil Griffin; Stockard Channing as Cynthia Griffin;
Marcia Gay Harden as Dr. Leslie Rosen; Victor
Garber as Bill Atchison; Elizabeth Berkley as
Phoebe LaVelle; Bronson Pinchot as Duarto
Feliz

Olivia Goldsmith's bestseller
turned into the surprise
smash-hit movie of 1996.

SYNOPSIS

When Cynthia Griffin commits suicide because her husband has dumped her for a younger "trophy" wife, her three school chums—Brenda, Elise, and Annie—reunite for her funeral. When the three realize that they, like Cynthia, have been shunted aside by their ungrateful husbands who have gone after younger women, they decide to seek justice. They form "the First Wives Club" and plot to get back at their wayward exes. They succeed dramatically: Annie writes a book about their ordeal, Elise reclaims her career with a big Broadway hit, Brenda considers taking back her contrite hubby, and together they create a women's shelter.

REVIEWS

"The First Wives Club *represents the dumbing down, into a lowbrow comedy, of a woman's reasonable anger about being dumped for a younger partner by her husband. . . . Put such veteran stars as Goldie Hawn, Bette Midler, and Diane Keaton into such an emotional plight and one could hope for a biting social comedy on the order of, say,* Shampoo *(1975). But American movies have gone soft in the last two decades, and what we get in* The First Wives Club *is basically material for coming attractions and TV ads: the girls singing together, dancing together, and falling together on a scaffold outside an unfaithful husband's new apartment. Oh, the stories Hawn, Midler, and Keaton could tell about men. But we never get to hear them. . . . it's high jinks as they plot revenge, get the money and, in a throwaway that seems totally insincere, set up a shelter for abused women."*

—GENE SISKEL, *CHICAGO TRIBUNE*

"Bette Midler, Diane Keaton, and Goldie Hawn make a spirited, surprisingly harmonious trio. They reel off one-liners with accomplished flair, even when the film turns silly and begins to, pardon the expression, sag. As directed by Hugh Wilson (Police Academy, Guarding Tess) *and written by Robert Harling (*Soapdish *and* Steel Magnolias), *it fares better with sight gags and quick retorts than with plot development. There's a lot to enjoy here, but the ladies wind up sanctimoniously opening a women's crisis center and romping through a girl-group musical number that's painful to see."*

—JANET MASLIN, *NEW YORK TIMES*

When *The First Wives Club* opened on September 20, 1996, it took America by storm. The film received some good—and many not-so-good—reviews. Paramount Pictures projected that it would bring in about $8 million on its opening weekend. When the receipts revealed that it had taken in nearly $20 million—the biggest opening ever for a nonholiday September release—Paramount knew they had a smash on their hands. Bette would later boast about it in the *Diva Las Vegas* parody number "Everything's Comin' Up Grosses!"

The success of **The First Wives Club** *was reflected in the media with covers on* **People, Time,** *and* **Ladies Home Journal.**

Things look swell,
Things look great,
I got 20 percent of the gate.
Who'd have dreamt?
I'm verklempt!
'Cause everything's coming up
grosses!
At the top,
In my prime.
On the cover of People *and*
Time!
Scrape and bow, when I pass.
Blow some smoke, up my ass.
One hundred million, ain't so
hard to do.
Honey, everything's coming up
grosses for me
So fuck you!

First Wives went on to become the only certified all-female $100 million blockbuster ever. What was it about this picture that touched a chord with audiences? The theme of justice had something to do with it, and many magazine articles tried to suggest that the story of discarded first wives resonated for women around the world. Goldie Hawn, Diane Keaton, and Bette were soon on the cover of *People* and *Time; First Wives* was a sensation.

Certainly the success of Olivia Goldsmith's bestseller, coupled with the superb, superstar casting of Midler, Hawn, and Keaton, had a lot to do with *The First Wives Club* phenomenon. But so did timing. It came out in the middle of a horrendous drought of good films, and its topicality and star power were so strong that it captivated audiences.

Despite what Hollywood gossips might have hoped, there was no dissension or temperament among the three stars. The women bonded during the filming of The *First Wives Club* and became good friends. It was like a mutual admiration society, each woman appreciating the accomplishment of the others. As each of them celebrated their fiftieth birthday during the shoot, they partied together. When all was said and done, *The First Wives Club* was serendipity for the superstar trio, and they knew it.

In the end, these first wives have bonded and prospered.

That Old Feeling

Universal, 1997

CREDITS:
Producers: Bonnie Bruckheimer and Leslie Dixon; Director: Carl
Reiner; Screenplay: Leslie Dixon; Cinematographer: Steven Mason;
Film Editor: Richard Halsey; Costumes: Robert DeMora;
Composer: Patrick Williams
MPAA Rating—PG-13; Running Time: 105 minutes

CAST:
Bette Midler as Lilly; Dennis Farina as Dan; Danny Nucci as Joey;
Gail O'Grady as Rowena; David Rasche as Alan; Jamie Denton as
Keith; Paula Marshall as Molly

SYNOPSIS

At the wedding of their conservative daughter, diva movie star Lilly
and her novelist ex-husband, Dan, rediscover their love. They run off
together, causing their spouses to flip out and to insist that the newly-
weds get them back. The action moves to Manhattan where the bride
enlists the help of a paparazzi photographer to track down her mother, and the two unexpectedly fall in love. In the end, Dan and Lilly
decide to stick together, and Molly leaves her uptight groom for the
photographer.

REVIEWS

*"She may not be your cup of vinaigrette, but Bette Midler knows who
she is, and what it is she should do: Walk loudly and carry a big
shtick. She's done it for a long time, and she does it well. And she's
seldom been more Bette than as the brassy, sassy, and lethally theatrical
Lilly of* That Old Feeling, *a shticky situational comedy that pays tribute to director Carl Reiner's roots in television while giving some well-
deserved exposure to a lot of talented people.* That Old Feeling *is a
very traditional comedy in a surreal sort of way. [It] is generally fun,
thanks to old pros Midler and Farina."*

—JOHN ANDERSON, *LOS ANGELES TIMES*

*"Usually, Bette Midler can save any film she stars in. But, despite top
billing, she is not the star of* That Old Feeling. *Instead, the movie
focuses on the character of her daughter (a young Daphne Zuniga type)
and a sleazy paparazzo (a young Tony Danza type). Ask yourself:*

Would you run out to see a comedy starring Daphne Zuniga and Tony Danza? That Old Feeling *is directed by that great comedy master Carl Reiner. And while it's good to see him active so late in the game, there is little here to suggest a genius at work. . . . This is tiresome, predictable, unfunny stuff. Molly and her paparazzo are not interesting characters and you have to wonder what a comedy guru like Reiner thinks he's doing—and why Bette Midler decided to appear in this film anyway. She does get to sing a song and wear some nice clothes. (She looks especially good in a bright turquoise outfit.) But there's not much for her to do but support the unsupportable. So you watch, and watch—and the film goes nowhere. The laughs are few and far between. And the movie does not contain one genuine emotion. It's pure (and poor) comedy product. At one point, things grow so desperate that the characters crash a Latino wedding for no other reason, it seems, than to pump a little energy into the background proceedings. It doesn't help. Both Bette Midler and Carl Reiner have been great in the past but, despite the film's title, that old feeling is exactly what's missing."*

—Lawrence Frascella, The *New York Times*

That Old Feeling was an All Girl Production that Bette and partner Bonnie Bruckheimer had in development for years. The romantic comedy, coming on the heels of the success of *The First Wives Club,* is the story of a couple who have been divorced for fourteen years, but who discover—at their daughter's wedding—that the old flame still burns. So, too, do the old arguments. In a mad moment, they flee the wedding and take off for a passionate escapade in New York.

Screenwriter Leslie Dixon, who wrote *Outrageous Fortune,* came up with the idea for *That Old Feeling* when she witnessed her long-divorced parents hitting it off at a family party. Bette told the *New York Times* that her character, Lilly, "is an actress's actress," (meaning self-absorbed, shallow, and out of touch with everything but her own publicity). "She's utterly selfish. There's a tiny transformation when she becomes minimally less selfish, but that's it." While this description makes Lilly seem less than likable, Bette felt otherwise: "She's what's known colloquially as a 'doll.' She's got her airs, but she's salt of the earth underneath it all. In her own harebrained little way, she's full of mischief and fun."

That Old Feeling was scheduled for release on Valentine's Day, but was switched to April for no explicable reason. The previous date—a tie in with the holiday—may have helped the picture, especially since the reviews for *That Old Feeling* were mediocre. Despite Bette coming off her biggest box office hit ever, *The First Wives Club,* audiences were not interested in *That Old Feeling*. The opening weekend grossed less than $5 million, and it never caught on. By Memorial Day, *That Old Feeling* was a distant memory to most filmgoers.

ADDITIONAL NOTES

In 1965, Bette, who was a student at the University of Hawaii, got her very first movie role. When George Roy Hill brought a Hollywood film crew to Honolulu to shoot scenes for the film adaptation of James Michener's bestseller *Hawaii,* Bette was cast in a nonspeaking bit part. Alongside stars Julie Andrews, Max von Sydow, and Gene Hackman, Bette played the wife of a missionary sailing from England to Honolulu. The role called for her to be seasick most of the time, with her head over the side of the ship, heaving. The film was released in 1966. Today, only the sharpest eyes can find Bette in the Hawaii-bound ship scenes.

A few years later—1971—while Bette was doing a singing engagement in Toronto, she was offered the role of the Virgin Mary in an irreverent spoof of the story of Jesus Christ called *The Greatest Story Ever Overtold*—on its initial release. Directed by Peter Alexander, it was a lame effort, unfunny and crude. Bette sings "I've Got a Date With an Angel," and plays Mary as a promiscuous ditz. Her screen time is less than fifteen minutes, but that didn't stop producers from trying to re-release the film in 1974 to take advantage of Bette's fame by calling it *The Divine Mr. J,* a take-off on her Divine Miss M moniker. Their misleading ad campaign was thwarted by Aaron Russo, who sued to force them to change the advertising. A few years later, the film was released on home video and called *The Thorn*.

SIX

Best-Laid Plans

Bette Midler is the kind of larger-than-life personality who was made for the big screen—the movies. Ever since she burst on the scene in 1972, even before she ever made *The Rose*, she's been mentioned in association with dozens of movie projects. In many cases, these films were merely gossip or conjecture. Occasionally, attaching Bette's name to a proposed picture was simply wishful thinking. Sometimes it was a good idea that may still be in the works. Here is a collection of productions that have yet to see the light of day . . . but may tomorrow.

Absolutely Fabulous

Britain's funniest—and most depraved—TV comedy, which starred Jennifer Saunders and Joanna Lumley as Edina Monsoon and Patsy Stone, two over-the-hill divas still into cocaine, pills, booze, and excess. It was once proposed as a feature film with Bette as Eddie and Goldie Hawn as Patsy. This is not to be confused with a Roseanne-proposed American TV series, which never came to pass either.

An Actor's Life for Me

The story of screen star Lillian Gish when she was a child actress at the turn of the century. Disney turned it down.

Annie Get Your Gun

Like *Mame* and *Anything Goes*, this is another classic musical that was discussed for Bette after *Gypsy*. *Annie Get Your Gun*, the story of sharp-shooter Annie Oakley and her romance with Frank Butler, includes

Bette Midler's name has been attached to dozens of projects.

the hit songs "Anything You Can Do I Can Do Better," "They Say That Falling in Love Is Wonderful," and "There's No Business Like Show Business." Bette said of this Irving Berlin show, "I'd like to do all those kind of broad parts, you know. I feel bad that the nation doesn't get to celebrate this tradition more often. It's valuable, something we should be proud of."

The Rose *was Bette's first film, and she's searched for years to find something that good again.*

Anything Goes

The classic Cole Porter musical, most recently staged on Broadway in the 1980s with Patti Lupone. After the success of *Gypsy*, *Anything Goes* was talked about as a possible follow-up.

Autograph

The life of an autograph hunter, based on the novel by Arnold Schulman (*Funny Lady, A Hole in the Head*).

Avon Ladies of the Amazon

A comedy based on a *People* article that revealed that the fastest-growing market for Avon cosmetics was in the Amazon jungle. Originally, it was a *Romancing the Stone* kind of comedy about a woman who gets stranded up the Amazon. After the success of *The First Wives Club*, producers proposed reteaming Bette, Diane Keaton, and Goldie Hawn and sending all three of them up the river. The script was written by Jane Anderson, who also wrote the Emmy-winning TV movie *The Positively True Adventures of the Alleged Texas Cheerleader-Murdering Mom* for HBO. The latter was directed by Michael Ritchie (*Divine Madness*).

Down and Out in Beverly Hills **Sequel**

What happened to the Whitemans and Jerry Baskin in the turbulent 1990's? That's the premise of the proposed sequel to the Disney hit of 1986. Of course, to reunite Bette, Nick Nolte, and Richard Dreyfuss, Disney will have to pay considerably more than it did back then when the studio "saved" their floundering careers.

The Dorothy Parker Story

A proposed biography of the cynical poet and author who was part of the famous Algonquin Round Table. Jennifer Jason Leigh played Parker in the 1994 film *Mrs. Parker and the Vicious Circle*, emphasizing Parker's unhappy love life.

The Divine Miss M Movie

Yes, even the Divine has been talked about as a possible big-screen adventure.

Dreamer

A biography of the late singer Bobby Darin, to be directed by Barry Levinson and written by Lorenzo Carcaterra (*Sleepers*). Reportedly, Levinson was interested in Johnny Depp playing Darin, with Drew Barrymore as his wife, actress Sandra Dee. Bette Midler would have the integral role of Darin's sister, Nina.

Dry Hustle

Based on Sarah Kernochan's novel about two Times Square dance parlor hustlers. Bette described it as "a kind of female *Midnight Cowboy.*"

Emma Goldman

A biography based on the life of the 1920s American labor activist and anarchist.

Faye & Artie

Written by Anne Meara, it is a comedy about a husband who's a famous star and the wife who is the real power behind him, writing his material for years and never getting any credit.

The Fortune Cookie

A proposed remake of Billy Wilder's 1966 comedy. The update would pair Bette Midler and Candice Bergen in roles originally played by Walter Matthau and Jack Lemmon. Matthau won an Oscar as Whiplash Willie, a shyster lawyer who sees dollar signs when his brother-in-law, a TV cameraman, is run over by a superstar athlete while shooting a football game. The lawyer convinces him to exaggerate the injuries for insurance purposes.

Green Acres

For 20th Century Fox, a big-screen adaptation of the vintage TV sitcom, with Bette in the role of Lisa Douglas, which was originally played by Eva Gabor. *Green Acres* ran for six years on CBS beginning in 1965. It's the story of Oliver Wendell Douglas and his wife Lisa, who leave the posh life of New York society for the simple joys of farm life. "Since Bette is the acknowledged queen of composting, it's only fitting she should play a role like this," said Bonnie Bruckheimer, Bette's All Girl Productions partner.

Hello, Suckers!

The long-planned biography of Texas Guinan, the bawdy nightclub owner from the wild roaring twenties. As of 1996, Bette and director Martin Scorsese had a deal going at Universal to make the picture, using Louise Berliner's book, *Texas Guinan: Queen of the Nightclubs.*

How High the Moon?

The story of 1940s big-band leader Ina Ray Hutton and her all-girl band. The script for the film has been written by Linda Bloodworth-Thomason (of *Designing Women* fame).

Isn't She Great?

Bette would play novelist Jacqueline Susann (*Valley of the Dolls*) in this adaptation of Michael Korda's *New Yorker* piece about his early career working as an assistant to the diva authoress. Reportedly, Andrew Bergman would direct, Mike Lobell would produce, and TriStar would release the film.

The Jazz Band Ball

A musical set in 1948 to 1952, when swing music was replaced by bop.

Ladyfingers

A comedy scheduled to be filmed in 1997.

Leading With My Heart

An adaptation of Virginia Kelley's autobiography, recounting her life long before her son, Bill Clinton, became president of the United States.

Legends

Proposed project for Barbra Streisand and Bette about two great actresses who team up for the first time and the problems that arise. Carol Channing and Mary Martin played the roles in 1986 in its original incarnation, the James Kirkwood play *The Diary of a Mad Playwright*.

Little Me

A film version of the Broadway musical, which was an adaptation of Patrick Dennis's comic novel telling of the adventures of Belle Poitrine. Neil Simon wrote the play, with music by Cy Coleman and Carol Leigh, including the hit "I Got Your Number."

Lotte Lenya

All Girl Productions and Storyline Productions (Craig Zadan and Neil Meron) planned this biopic for TriStar. The story would cover the life of the famed German singer who was married to composer Kurt Weill. In 1991, Bette revealed, "That is a very dark story, and very interesting. They [Lenya and Weill] had an open marriage and she was his muse, in a way. He died and she made it her life's work to keep his music from dying. She's quite a wonderful character."

Mame

After the success of *Gypsy*, there was talk about Bette starring in a TV version of the Jerry Herman Broadway smash *Mame*, a musical version of *Auntie Mame*. *Mame* follows the same story, telling of Patrick Dennis's childhood adventures with his eccentric aunt.

My Fair Larry

A musical, role-reversal version of *My Fair Lady* (which is a musical version of George Bernard Shaw's *Pygmalion*), with Bette as a fashion executive who tries to turn a janitor into her perfect man. Eventually, she falls in love with him.

Murdering Mr. Monti

A comedy based on Judith Viorst's book.

My Girdle Is Killing Me

Based on a screenplay by Peter Dallas. He told James Spada in *The Divine Bette Midler* that it's the story of "a lovable and naive movie star who hits the skids and is penniless when the telegram arrives that she has been nominated for an Oscar. Then it's a scramble for the bucks so she can get herself to Hollywood and present herself like a star."

Palm Beached

Based on the story of jet-setter Molly Wilmot, who gained notoriety when a Venezuelan freighter came to rest alongside her Palm Beach swimming pool in 1984. Touchstone's story line called for the socialite to feed caviar and paté to a comical Venezuelan crew from the stranded freighter.

The Polish Nightingale

A comedy set in the 1930s about a singer.

The Return of Magda La Silva

Based on Albert Innaurato's off-Broadway play, it's the story of an opera singer's return to her South Philly neighborhood.

Scrambled Eggs

A comedy developed by All Girl Productions about two women—one white and one African-American—who are pregnant at the same time.

The Shirelles Story

A movie about the creation of the Shirelles, the 1960s girl group. They were discovered by Florence Greenberg, a New Jersey housewife. Bette would play Greenberg, who also became the president of the record label and produced the girls' albums. Eddie Murphy's production company is interested in co-producing with All Girl Productions, and En Vogue would play the Shirelles. Among the Shirelles' hits were "Dedicated to the One I Love," "Soldier Boy," and "Will You Still Love Me Tomorrow?"

Show Business Kills
Based on the bestseller by Iris Rainer Dart (*Beaches*), it's the story of four over-forty women in Hollywood, of stars and those married to stars.

The Sophie Tucker Story
A proposed biography of the famed "red-hot mama" songstress.

Strike and Hyde
A zany comedy with Bette as a Hawaiian woman named Leslie Strike who goes to Las Vegas to become a comic. There she meets a New York psychiatrist named Norman Hyde, who has come to Vegas to lecture Gamblers Anonymous about his new book—*The Self-Destructive Ape.* Leslie falls in love with Norman, while Norman's wife, seeing her marriage failing, runs off with a black lounge singer.

Untitled Murder-Mystery Comedy
The story of a female detective who becomes a stand-up comic.

Traps
A thriller, with music, which Bette is developing as an NBC-TV movie.

Tulku
An action-adventure story set at the turn of the century about a music hall singer who goes to China at the time of the Boxer Rebellion on a botanical expedition. She befriends a half-Chinese boy whose minister father is murdered.

A View From a Broad
In 1987, Bette talked about doing a low-budget film based on her successful—and fanciful—account of her 1979 world concert tour.

Welcome to the Family
Based on a script by Eric Idle (of the Monty Python comedy ensemble). In *Welcome*, Bette would play an obsessive mother who doesn't want her son to get married, so she schemes to sabotage the wedding.

Widows
Scenarist Richard LaGravanese's (*The Fisher King, The Mirror Has Two Faces*) caper about three women who finish off the bank heist planned by their now-dead husbands.

After **Gypsy,** *producers proposed* **Mame, Anything Goes,** *and* **Annie Get Your Gun** *for Bette. (Tony Esparza/CBS)*

Annie

Ray Stark's adaptation of the long-running Broadway hit was filled with topnotch talent: Albert Finney, Tim Curry, Bernadette Peters, Ann Reinking. Stark wanted Bette, but settled for Carol Burnett. According to Bette, she wasn't sure she could handle the role: "They wanted me for Miss Hannigan, the villainess you love to hate. I didn't know if I could do that. I just thought they'd hate me."

Foul Play

Goldie Hawn very capably played the role in Colin Higgins's caper comedy, Chevy Chase's first feature as a leading man. Considering that Bette said yes to *Jinxed,* a similar kind of comedy, this one would have been better. *Foul Play* featured a Barry Manilow theme song—"Ready to Take a Chance Again."

The Fortune

The most celebrated opportunity that Bette let get by. In retrospect, it was the right move. Stockard Channing played the role of a girl who is seduced by Warren Beatty and then kidnapped by Beatty and Jack Nicholson in this tired, badly conceived farce. According to Bette, she never even managed to be auditioned for the role. "I was supposed to have a meeting with Mike Nichols and I was late for it because I'd been attacked by this masseur. And he [Nichols] was mad at me: first because I was late; secondly because he had to deal with my manager at the time [Russo] who must have given him an earful; and thirdly because I was so rattled at the time I didn't even know who I was talking to. So he never forgave me. To this day, I've never done a Mike Nichols picture." Mike Nichols may have Oscar credits to his name, but *The Fortune* wasn't one of them. It was a major flop for him, and Bette was better off without it.

King Kong

Was it because Bette did the first-act finale of *Clams on the Half-Shell* in King Kong's palm that producers imagined her doing it for real? The role of the woman who stirs the loins of the great ape eventually went to Jessica Lange. The movie was a bomb, so Bette was better off out of Dino DeLaurentis's jungle epic.

Misery

Bette passed on the part, but was very happy for Kathy Bates, who won the role . . . and an Oscar for her performance. Bette admitted on *Arsenio Hall* that she was afraid to play the role of an obsessed fan who saves—then imprisons—her favorite fiction writer. "What would the fans think?" she wondered. Ironically, her *For the Boys* costar, James Caan, played the victimized writer.

Nashville

Bette was slated for the Barbara Harris role—i.e., an Albuquerque housewife who's an aspiring country-western singer—in the Robert Altman film. It was one of Altman's landmark movies. Bette probably should have done it.

Rocky

Yo, Bette! Can you see Bette in the nerdy glasses and wool hat as Adrienne? It seems far-fetched now, but before Talia Shire got the role, it was offered to Bette. In 1980—four years after *Rocky* had won the Oscar as Best Picture—Bette commented: "One supporting role I should have taken, if my then-manager hadn't turned it down, was the Talia Shire role in *Rocky*. I'd still like to work with Sylvester Stallone. There's something about those beefy Italians that turns me on. But when he sent over the *Rocky* screenplay, my manager told me it was a nice role, a nice movie, but not for me." Bette is right about the role not being right for her, but there's no saying it wouldn't have been reworked for Bette's unique abilities.

Sister Act

A Disney-concocted comedy that turned into box office gold for Whoopi Goldberg. It was actually written for Bette, but for a variety of reasons—primarily, the disappointment over *For the Boys*—she passed. The story about a Reno lounge singer who witnesses a murder and then hides out in a convent was one of the biggest hits of 1992, spawning a far less successful follow-up, *Sister Act 2*. It's possible that Bette was inured to the formulaic Disney material at the time, but if she had recognized the long-running success of *Nunsense*—the off-Broadway comedy hit—she would have taken *Sister Act* and done wonders with it.

Straight Talk

The story of a down-home girl who becomes a radio pop psychologist despite no professional expertise. Bette was offered the role, as were Goldie Hawn and Julia Roberts, before Disney decided to fashion it for Dolly Parton. It was a major flop.

Won Ton Ton, the Dog That Saved Hollywood

This strained, stupid all-star comedy was a failed satire of 1920s Hollywood. Madeline Kahn took the role Bette—wisely—turned down.

"Every time I get up there it's magic time."

SEVEN

In Her Own Words

According to Bette Midler, "Everything I've said in interviews is *bush-wah,* you know. There's not a kernel of truth in any of them, and they're all so repetitive." Yes, well, that may be, but many of the things Bette Midler has said in twenty-five years of interviews paint a fascinating portrait of a woman who knows all about stardom, celebrity, power, love, sex, and a myriad of other issues.

Here's the inimitable Divine Miss M, in her own words, on . . .

LIFE

"It's very dangerous to believe all the things they say about you. You can't be swept off your feet by it because it's not the truth, it's not everyday life. It doesn't have anything to do with being a human being. It has to do with being above the ordinary mortal. Real life is not like that. Anyway, I did it all for my own satisfaction, to see if I could do it. To see if anyone could understand it if I put it in front of them, to see if there was anyone else out there who was dreaming the same dreams I was dreaming."

"I compartmentalize my life now. I don't let my businesses flow into my personal life, where before it was all pretty much one thing. I am crazy about my child, and I don't want my profession to affect her in any adverse way. I also work a lot faster now because I simply don't have the time to go through some languorous process where I agonize over every song and every decision."

"I have to create. I have to dig in the earth. I have to make something grow. I have to bake something. I have to write something. I have to sing something. I have to put something out. It's not a need to prove anything. It's just my way of life."

"I'm more world-weary than I once was. I don't think the world is such a great place anymore. It was once simpler, and more private, and cleaner, and people had more respect for each other."

"I'm very glad that I've lived the life that I live. It [has] made me what I am. I'm having a fabulous time."

"I hold a grudge, absolutely. I just don't need my enemies any longer. When I was younger, I needed them. I was mad, and I'm not even sure why I was so mad. It's from when I was a kid. It got me through many, many years in New York, that anger, from like 1965 to 1975. Ten years of it, and I grew out of it. This [success] is like a major payback. I used all the anger. I've really used it all up."

"My public image is bold, brazen, intelligent, witty, sarcastic, bright, bawdy, take no prisoners, fly in the face of convention, noise, noise, noise. Who am I really? I'm the waif sitting in the corner, the shriveled-up little waif, the little worm in the corner."

"There's a certain kind of pomposity that I cannot bear, and most people from the class of people I come from—I mean, I'm not a blueblood, I just come from the worst class—really like to see the bubble burst. They like to see that the emperor has no clothes. And it's one of my favorite things to do. Bursting bubbles. Disrobing the emperor. Of course, one of these days, somebody's bound to say this empress is wearing no clothes, too."

HER APPEAL

"People come to see me because they want to be entertained. I just happen to be very loose about myself . . . free . . . I feel I can do anything. And I do. People have given me liberty and I make use of that. On stage, you have to take chances. You have to find new life for yourself. I'll do anything that keeps me alive, that keeps my face alive, that keeps my heart beating. That's what people pay money for. They pay money to see people do things they can't do or would not do."

"I'm not funny—I'm completely hysterically funny. When I'm

inspired, I'm untouchable. No one can top me. But I don't find life funny anymore. Not with the hatred in this country, not with the terrible toll AIDS has taken, not with the amount of ugliness in the world."

HER LOOKS

"I'm not traditionally beautiful, but I'm sexy."

"My looks have been limiting for me, but I think I've survived it very well. Because of my looks, I don't think anyone ever thought of me as a leading lady. I've convinced them I can be a kind of leading lady, though not the ordinary kind. I've gone around the back door, through broad comedy."

"Everybody asks me whether I'm going to have a nose job. I ask myself, too. I've thought of it but I won't give in. I know why but I can't decide if the reason is good or bad. I don't think it would be a bad idea—I don't think it would hurt my looks any. But I'd be real embarrassed if people knew that I did it. It's not really that bad . . . I don't know. To me, altering the way you look goes somewhere else, it's a whole other realm of thought. I always thought strangely about people who have altered themselves. No. I don't think I'll have a nose job."

"If you're going to bring up now how I'm not pretty, I've had enough of that, too. . . . Well, I have my look. I used to be quite sensitive

"I've always liked songs that tell stories, partly because I'm an actor."

about that 'not pretty' stuff, but not so much anymore. I'm having too good a time."

"Sometimes I think I'm in the wrong era. Yet I know I'm lucky to be where I am because then I would never have made the cut. I don't have the face for it, and I don't have the body. I don't have anything they required except the enthusiasm and the drive."

"I can look much smaller than I really am. Ten pounds is death to me—death! I get so fed up with dieting and exercising, so I put those pounds on fast. People who meet me when I'm not working think I'm short and fat. It's like a whole other person—the true me, the me who was supposed to be. But I can't let anyone see it because it's too shocking, too shocking!"

"I was an ugly, fat little Jewish girl with problems. I kept trying to be like everybody else, but on me nothing worked."

HER FAMILY

"[My father] really thought I would never amount to anything, but I said to myself, 'Oh, yeah? I'll show you!' My father was very conservative, and I remember saying 'darn' once and having my mouth washed out. But, oh, he was funny and really a laugh junkie. . . . I had a fabulous mother. She made me believe in myself, and I used a lot of her in the film [*Stella*]. She was not a single parent like Stella, but we were poor and she was that generation of women, almost all gone now, who always put their family ahead of themselves. She worked hard and kept nothing for herself, nothing. Never a new dress or new shoes. She adored me, my mom, and I still have nightmares about her, because as a grown-up, I didn't give her the time I should have. Now that she's gone, I have regrets. Even if I didn't like the style of the life they chose to live—their clothes, the furniture—she and my father were impeccable about teaching the value of things: to be honest, to have compassion and find the worth in people instead of looking for negatives."

"I miss my folks sometimes. You never get over death. It just becomes part of your scar tissue, part of your armor, and part of you. . . . I think about my sister [Judith] and I often wonder how we would be now. You never get over it; I don't think you should get over it. If it impedes you or if you find yourself disintegrating and unable to go on, then you should get over it, but otherwise I think it enriches your life to be able to say: 'This is the relationship I had with my family.' Especially if you finished your business with them. I was not able to with my mother, but with my father I was. I took care of him and visited him a lot during his last couple of years, and we came to our peace."

"Judith, who was the most brilliant, perceptive, sensitive person, came to New York then [in 1968] to join me and to study to become a moviemaker. She had lived there for only three months when she was killed in a traffic accident while on her way to meet me at the theater. That was more than twenty years ago. I think about her—I miss her—every day of my life."

"I like fighting. I guess I always thought it was sexy for women to fight. My father was a bellower. My sister and I fought night and day, though we loved each other."

"I have a brother, Daniel, who

got the measles when he was very young—six months or so—and had a terribly high fever. And my mother didn't give him the right aspirin or something, and he had brain damage. After that, my parents' lives were centered on building up a nest egg so Daniel could live on his own and not have to go into a city shelter. My father worked seven days a week, no vacations. I don't think my parents did the wrong thing for Daniel. Today he has a speech defect and little seizures, but he's in seventh heaven. He lives by himself. I mean he has thousands of friends. He has a job. He's very smart. We lost my older sister in a freak accident. She was a genius, and the most bitter woman I have ever encountered in my life. I loved my mother. She worked from dawn to dark taking care of us, and she was kind of bitter, too. My parents never shared any feelings with us. I sensed that my mother was crazy about my father, but my father was a real withholding kind of guy. I don't remember a single time he ever gave her a kiss."

"Being Danny's sister has made me different from everybody

"I'm having a fabulous time!"

In her New York apart-
ment prior to her HBO
special Art or Bust!
(UPI/Corbis-Bettman)

156

else, and I'd never trade it in. Knowing the depth of pain and frustration—his and my parents'—has made me what I am."

HER DAUGHTER, SOPHIE

"Sophie's my number one priority. I have the best child. We had a rough patch there in the terrible twos when she learned the word 'no,' but she is very like me. She speaks her mind and has a strong will. Some shyness, too. She'll stand outside a circle and watch people, rather than joining in. Which is the way I am. . . . I'm going to teach her she can do anything she can think of doing. She's as good as anybody, and nobody can stop her."

"What I'm really interested in is whether my five-year-old daughter finds me enchanting. Just watching her experience her growing pains, see new things in a brand-new way—a new trick on the jungle gym—it's really thrilling. It's the strongest, closest love I've ever had in my whole life."

HER MARRIAGE

"Artists are selfish people, and I had to learn not to be quite so selfish, and I think it [marriage] helps everything. It helps one's art, because it brings balance to it and it brings perspective and makes one quieter and able to judge in a less hysterical fashion."

"[Martin and I] are the perfect couple even though we go at it hammer and tongs. We're solid together."

"It's very hard to pay attention to your career and have enough time to put into your marriage. In your career, the bigger you get, the more the business end creeps up on you. . . . Suddenly, you turn around and you're entangled in these webs of deals and situations and obligations and places you have to be. And if you're not really careful, you can have no private life left."

HAWAII

"In Hawaii, the sky is very high and bright blue, and the scent of flowers, of plumeria, would hang in the breeze, caressing you, smelling so good coming down from the mountains—the real purple mountain majesties. And the beams of sun would shoot out of the banks of pristine clouds, and you just knew there was a God and that He had made all this just for you."

"I'm a walking dichotomy. Though my image is urban, brash, fast, I have sugar-cane roots. It's a part of myself I cherish."

"Remember the notion of solipsism from philosophy? Well, sometimes I think I'm dreaming the whole thing. Like today I was flying in a private plane, and the limo came to the tarmac to pick me up. But it's me, Bette. I'm from Hawaii, from AIEA. And I lived next to the dumpster! Being a star doesn't reconcile with who's living inside me. My husband says my life is wasted on me."

"We lived in a fabulous place called Halauua Housing—poor people's housing. At the time I really hated it—I was an alien, a foreigner even though I was born there—but now I have very fond memories of it. The kids in the neighborhood were Hawaiians, part Hawaiians, Samoans, and Filipinos."

"I've always been considered an urban artist, as in someone who comes from a big city. But I don't come from a big city. I come from a small town. I walked five miles to school every day from the time I was thirteen. I mean, I know rural."

LOVE

"I love to be in love. I'm always very happy and I do my best work when I'm in love. But I happen to have a lot of trouble with relationships—you know, male-female relationships—and I can't figure it out. I'm really a child of the media and I always believed those stories, those images in the movies and on TV. That's why I do what I do when I get involved with people, and it doesn't seem to work. I figured all that stuff was drawn from life, and now I can't figure out why life isn't like that. So now I'm trying to unlearn those lies and find out what the truth is."

SEX

"I never fake orgasm. Never, never. Never had to."

"People are people, elephants are elephants. You don't hate a group of people just because that's the way they choose to have sex."

"I have hooker fantasies that can be traced back to the time I was growing up outside Honolulu. On Saturdays, my sister and I would go into town. We'd go out to the red-light district and wander around. It was such a sexy place. All the sailors and other servicemen would go there to see a dirty movie or a bawdy show or to pick up a girl. It was a real red-light district—with opium dens and lots of Orientals—and it was so wonderful. And the prostitutes seemed so glamorous to me. I'd try to imagine the romantic, exotic lives I was sure they led. Later, when I became a singer and began doing concerts, I was able to act out my hooker fantasies on stage."

MONEY

"I'll tell you how poor we were. I slept on rags. I never had a towel that wasn't patched. It was just squalid."

"I am quite cheap. I don't own shopping centers, I don't have any tax shelters, I don't have stock in any bank, I don't do any wheeling and dealing. But I can get very agitated, and I can say, 'Where's the money?' I'm interested to see how they work these schemes in business. And then when I find out, I want to practically throw myself on a funeral pyre, because I think, 'Oh my God, I'm broke.' But I'm conservative about money because I see constant waste around me. People are so damned mindless, brainwashed almost, about buying up everything. People want to be on the top of the trend. With these leveraged buyouts, stock market gambits, and ways of buying money, people are just going nuts."

FRIENDSHIP

""I've found that friendships between two women and those between a gay man and a woman are closer than those a woman could have with a straight man. Straight men don't have time to spend with you because they have to get laid, they have to work, and if they're married, they have to keep their marriages together. But with women, you can be your true self and not that face you put on."

SHOW BUSINESS SUCCESS

"I wanted to be a phenomenon, I didn't want to be just a schlepper."

"Every time I get up there it's magic time."

"I know that most of what I have is ephemeral. I also have a mind and want to have a life of the mind. This business isn't about acquiring stuff, about wearing fancy clothes or diamonds. Once you realize that it's about perceptions and ideas and the world, you're not interested in the really cheesy trappings of success."

"Sometimes I was sorry I had ever gotten swept up in it. Remember when Pinocchio goes to Stromboli, convinced he wants to be an actor? After Pinocchio performs, Stromboli puts him in a cage.

Well, that's what it's like. You want to do it; you're fascinated by the dream. But when you get there, you suddenly find that you're in a cage."

"I've learned how to negotiate and that some things are more important than others. In order to get what you want, you have to choose what's important. You have to find the point past which you would never go."

"Everyone's who's successful—the biggest, the highest, the best—believes that at bottom they are secretly a fraud. You always think that somebody's gonna find that out and take all this away. Anyway—I'm probably the only person in show business who doesn't say, 'I have to thank God for this.' Well, sure, I thank God, but I worked pretty hard at it, too."

"I'm not surprised [by success] because I know I have it. I have what it takes. I'm a hard worker, too. But I'm surprised at the strength of the popularity. Or not so much surprised as relieved. Not to be in the unemployment line. You don't ever forget that phase of your life."

"I really don't even feel I deserve all this. I have been a very lucky girl. Now I'm working and doing good work and loving it. I'm not going to say, 'Woe is me.' I can't. I'm too happy that anybody noticed I had any talent at all."

"It never occurred to me that I could fail. So, of course, I never made any alternative plans. Oh, there was a time when I considered being a foreign diplomat. But I didn't think they were appointing women to that sort of post then . . . and besides, I wasn't very diplomatic."

"I don't think of myself as a star. I wish I could. I had fantasies about getting there, but I never had any about what I would do when I got there. I'm sort of in the lurch about how to behave."

"I intended to be a movie star because I thought it was the high end. I thought it was where the work would survive, that if you had something beautiful and good to offer, it was worth the effort. I still feel that way, but not as strongly. Because I know how hard it is to make something good and beautiful. With your own personal vision. You almost have to be a giant of some sort."

PERFORMING LIVE

"When you really tell the truth—or sing the truth—and people receive it as the truth, and it changes something in their perspective, that's the

greatest thing of all, and that's the only reason I do it."

"I think I'm always on the edge between laughter and tears. I'm very emotional. I'm not happy with a performance, even acting, unless I feel I have been through something myself. In other words, I have to have a catharsis in order to be satisfied. And on stage, if you don't phony it up, if you don't disguise what you're feeling, then it's mesmerizing."

"I always felt strange and always felt the only way to get any kind of love at all was through performing. I never said it out loud to myself, but by the end of high school I had entrenched myself into performing very heavily. . . . I was always working on a show or some kind of presentation."

"When I started out, most people thought I was utter slime. They thought, 'Ughh, this person! Her act is so blue.' But the reason it was blue was that nobody else was doing that kind of material then, and I thought it was fun. Underneath, my virtue was intact. But then everybody else started doing blue material, and I thought, 'Ooh, who wants to be like everybody else?'"

"[On stage, I am] a character without fear, who has no prob-

At the 54th Academy Awards
(UPI/Corbis-Bettman)

lem being vulgar and outrageous. But in my private life, I'm one of the most paranoid persons in the world."

"I've got all these crazy characters living inside me, and I always have to act them out. Most people think I'm nuts."

"I show my dreams. I am more upfront about my fantasies. And the dreams and fantasies are more important to me than they are to a lot of people."

"I'm very lucky to have found my thing. I cannot fathom people doing for years what they hate. I think if you look hard enough you're going to find something you like to do. I work like a dog, but I'm lucky to be able to."

"I don't mind that people think I'm unusual. I really like that. But I don't want people to think I am an object of derision. I've been compared to Tiny Tim. I don't think of myself as anything like Tiny Tim, even vaguely, except that occasionally I pick a tune that is a little obscure and old. That's what labels like 'kookie' do to you. That word absolutely makes me nauseous."

"Being Danny's sister has made me different . . . and I'd never trade it in." (Nancy Barr/Retna Ltd.)

BEING A WOMAN IN HOLLYWOOD

"The business is run by men, and they're basically interested in their own species, and they're not so interested in women belonging to the human race. It's not that there's a conspiracy. There's a rising mediocrity, and women are the victims of it. The industry is an ecosystem that's sick. I made *Down and Out in Beverly Hills* eight or nine years ago, and since then I've read eight or nine scripts just like it. We need a broader menu."

"There's no trend. There are only individuals doing the best they can. To imagine that there's a trend or to try and find a trend is garbage! These are people whose fortunes wax and wane from picture to picture. I am one of them, and I can tell you, your stock is up one day and down the next. . . . As high as your star goes, that's as low as you sink. You can't stay up there forever."

"Most of us are so self-involved, looking at ourselves through a microscope. I'm always self-consciously prejudging, and judging my own actions."

"They used to make lists of the bankable girls, the girls who made the big bucks. I was never on anybody's list. It was like I was invisible. It was very upsetting."

"One has to be in charge of where one's career is going, but that's personal power. That's not getting other people to do what you want. On *Beaches* it was different because I was obliged to do more. But if I had my way, I wouldn't have said anything."

"The truth is that it pays not to care. It's better if you don't have your soul on the line. I haven't found anything that I'm ready to sell my soul for. If I do, I will, but I haven't yet. Not so far."

BROADWAY

"It was awful. I'll always love acting, but the hierarchy of Broadway and the treatment of professional people in that end of the business I don't care for, and I don't want to be involved again on the level I was involved last time."

"I started out as a musical performer, and I remain a musical performer in my heart of hearts. I waste my talent by not doing musicals of one sort or another."

MUSIC

"I think my albums are very special. I don't think they are technically the most perfect. They're raggedy. But I'm a raggedy performer. I don't want to ever be polished more than a little bit."

"I've always liked songs that tell stories, partly because I'm an actor. Actors don't want to keep on playing the same character, they want a chance to grow and stretch."

"Just the thought of music can really carry me away. I embarass people because I'll jump up and dance to 'Rock the Boat' if I hear it on the radio. Well, fortunately, I still get excited about what I do. The excitement of it all still carries me along. Every once in a while I think, 'Hallelujah, I'm still working.' "

"I think I was a black woman or a black man in another life. When I hear certain chords, I'm so affected by them. Sometimes I sob outright. Other times I hear a rhythm and I jump up. It doesn't matter what kind of party I'm at, I have to go off by myself and dance."

"What's the song? What's the experience of this particular song? Is it the message, or the arrangement, or the notes? Sometimes the theme of a piece is a style, sometimes it's a theatrical effect."

MAKING MOVIES

"It's so easy. If you do it wrong, they let you do it over again. On the stage, you have to go two hours straight without fucking up. I think it's lazy—no, not lazy, easy. You don't have to sweat and everyone is so sweet."

"The longer I do pictures, the more I wish I were on the stage. I especially think about it at six in the morning when they're slapping makeup on my face and pulling my hair. In the movies, you can wind up working nineteen hours a day. In the theater, you come in at 7:30, go on at 8 and come home at 11. You can have a life."

"Once I saw myself on the big screen and had my dream, I was simply lost. There was no new goal."

FILM DIRECTING

"Directing is just a bitch. It's years out of your life. And you are in a dark editing room a lot of it. You'd better like that person you are in there with because you're there, you're locked. It's a lot like making records. Sometimes it gets so claustrophic in those little dark rooms, it's hard. And I don't want to work that hard for no money."

THE CRITICS

"I made up my mind a long time ago . . . if you're gonna read the good, you gotta read the bad, too. And since I had no tolerance at all for even one bad word, even a suggestion, it became impossible for me to read not only reviews, but also any interviews that I had ever given."

"It's dangerous to read reviews—the good ones and the bad ones. I was crippled twice in my career by bad reviews, and I almost don't read them at all anymore. The bad ones hurt your feelings, and the good ones make you forget who you really are. They swell your head and they make you think your shit doesn't stink. When you stoop to that, whatever you had flies right out the window and you're just a shell. You're nothing."

PSYCHOTHERAPY

"When I was about nineteen, I went for a year, but I didn't get very much out of it. I finally had to go to another shrink so he could tell me how to get rid of the first shrink."

"I went to a shrink for a few months when I was twenty-two. He told me I was schizophrenic, so I didn't bother to go any further. Absolutely everyone, without question, has more than one side to him. Or her. I have a little girl who lives inside me who can't figure anything out. Then I have Bette Midler, who is very goal-oriented and business-minded. There's a side of me that hasn't got any confidence at all. And then there is the Divine, who has got all the self-confidence in the entire world. I adore her."

"Sometimes I think I should go into therapy. You can't imagine what it's like to live inside me with these emotions constantly beating at the gate. I look at other people and think they must be dead. I am definitely not dead, but I wish some of this stuff would lie down for a while."

DRUGS

"I don't do drugs. I have a devil. I don't get stoned because then it comes out and I can't control it and it's very sick. In my younger days, I smoked a lot of reefers, but I lost my voice so I stopped. I gave a lot of great shows, though—unfortunately, I croaked my way through them."

DOMESTICITY

"I'm a fabulous cook, and my husband is a fabulous cook. I collect cookbooks. I love good food. I sew. You won't believe it, but I sew. We decorate. We go to flea markets and swap meets. We have a lot of friends who own restaurants, people who like to eat well. I like that. There's a certain quality of life that's missing in this country. People go so fast—everything in this country is about speed, about going faster, having more status, more money. And I find that's not really the way."

REGRETS

"[I regret] tons of things. I regret making all those Karen Carpenter anorexia jokes. I cannot tell you how much I apologize. From the bottom of my soul, I apologize to her and her family. She had tremendous talent, and I was a jerk for saying those things. I was young and stupid and cruel and thought I was doing profound and enduring stuff. But I wasn't—I was adding to the ugliness of the world."

SENTIMENTALITY

"I think I have my feet in two worlds. One foot is in a bohemian, artsy downtown world and the other in a middle-class borough like Queens. It's the reason my musical tastes are so wide-ranging. My taste often goes to stuff that's almost maudlin. Lots of people are ashamed of their sentimental sides, but I'm not. My emotions are really close to the surface, and I'm easily affected by almost anything. I cry when the postman comes. I use that emotional openness to choose my material."

"I always try to balance the light with the heavy—a few tears for the human spirit in with the sequins and the fringes. One thing without the other is no good. People have great pain and great joy, and any time a performer comes out and stands up in front of an audience she has a moral obligation to be an entire human being instead of just half a human being."

EXCESS

"That's what's missing today. Decorum. I miss it. I miss rational, sensible people. I like to be outrageous, but I don't think everybody in the world should be."

"There are sixty channels on television. Sixty! It's too much! It's like going to Bloomingdale's. There are too many things in the world already, too much collecting, too much that's trivial, and not enough that's substantial."

"When I started out, I took sex and twisted it around to show its lighter side. Twenty years ago, I was the only person doing this, and it worked because it was unusual. But in recent years, the floodgates have opened, and the business has been taken over by low-life sluts. What ticks me off is that there's no originality left. Today, everyone is talking—and talking loudly—about nothing. Everything is watered-down, diluted junk inspired by the stupidity of television. Frankly, I find it pitiful and lousy."

"Television is toxic. For the most part, it is so horrible, so awful that it poisons everyone who looks at it. I hide it behind mirrors, behind doors, in closets."

AIDS

"If AIDS were a heterosexual disease, I have no doubt the federal government would be pumping much more money into research. I'm very, very angry when a company . . . that makes AZT won't lower the price. Making a profit off another human being's misery makes me wish I wasn't in the human race. Greed taints everything."

"I do try to help. If I didn't, I would really feel like I wasn't a human being. It's as though you were living in Nazi Germany during the Holocaust. What would you have done? How would you have behaved? I think most people don't perceive it as a holocaust because

Bette and Martin von Haselberg, her husband: "We're solid together." (Steve Granitz/Retna Ltd.)

many people are not touched. . . . I happen to be someone who is touched, every week, every month, every year for ten years."

"I'm grateful that people think I do a lot [about AIDS], but no matter what anyone is doing right now, it is not enough."

"The last ten years I have worked on behalf of people with AIDS because I couldn't stand idly by, twiddling my thumbs, pissing and moaning while people I loved shriveled up and died. I began my career in 1965, and I am not lying, I do not exaggerate one minute, when I tell you that nearly everyone who I started out with is dead. I never thought that at such a relatively young age I would be on such intimate terms with death. My whole adult life I have had gay friends, I've had gay collaborators, I've had gay mentors. And if I live to be a thousand, I could never repay the debt I owe to them. They gave me my vision and they gave me my career."

"I've lost everybody. I don't have any friends left—nobody to talk to. I know at least thirty-five men who have died from AIDS; dear, dear friends, three of them my dearest. I miss them . . . the laughs. Our culture is cruel, its homophobia unconscionable."

"I had this song, 'Friends,' and part of the lyric is *'I had good friends but they're gone/Something came and took them away/From the dusk till the dawn/Here is where I've stayed.'* That was one of the first songs I ever sang when I was at the Baths. And the song has followed me for twenty years now. And now it's like it was some kind of horrible prophecy that just came true. *'I had some friends but they're gone . . . something came and took them away.'* I just can't believe it. It's too close."

ARETHA FRANKLIN

"She was the reason I decided to sing . . . because she was pouring her heart out, musically, but she was also very dramatic. I mean, she might as well be an opera singer for all that. And I understood where she was coming from in terms of the drama. And that's what encouraged me to put my particular dramatic talent out there."

BARBRA STREISAND

"I think Barbra has one of the most beautiful pop voices. But I think her music doesn't mean as much to her as it once did. I think she wants to be a director. Barbra's looking for a different kind of respect than I am. I like her in a funny way; I'm not friends with her, but I'm not *not* friends. I've cooked for her."

MAE WEST

"I've always adored Mae West. I used to do her. I saw all her movies, and I have a whole stack of her records. That lady was a genius. She was a renegade, she was bold, she had such courage of her convictions. Such a life she led, and she wouldn't let anybody tell her not to. She just didn't care. She just stood up to all of them. She had her fantasy, and she made the world accept it. And that's what I'm doing."

PRINCE (a.k.a. the artist formerly known as Prince)

"I wish Prince would write me a song. I love those rock 'n' roll songs. Not all of them, not when it's too overtly sexy. I'm thinking more of 'Little Red Corvette,' that era. But even in my position, I'm very shy. It's hard for me to call and say, 'Please, will you write me a song?' "

BRUCE SPRINGSTEEN

"Another stiff. He wouldn't let me have a song. . . . It was 'Pink Cadillac' and Bruce wouldn't let me have it. I spent like $25,000 on the track and then he said I couldn't sing it: 'It wasn't a girl's song.' [Then] Natalie Cole cut it, after he recorded it. . . . I was going to record it before he did. But he wouldn't let me have it."

MEL BROOKS

"I worship Mel Brooks. My favorite of his is *The Producers.* I think it's the funniest movie ever made."

EIGHT

*B*est Bette:
On Stage

In twenty-five years in the spotlight, Bette Midler has emerged as the world's preeminent concert artist. Nobody is better than Bette on stage, in concert, under the lights, before an audience. As superb as she has been in other media—film, television, records, theater—it is live in concert that Midler has been most magical. It's nearly impossible to capture the special something that makes Bette so electrifying on stage, although TV specials, records, and feature films have tried. It remains the purest and most elusive quality that Bette has, and it will probably always be that way.

It began in the most unlikely of places—a gay bathhouse, a place where women weren't even welcome. The Continental Baths was not a tony, trendy, traditional venue. It was perhaps the strangest launching pad imaginable, but for a Jewish girl who had been brought up among Filipinos, Samoans, and Hawaiians in a Honolulu housing project, there was something oddly on-target about Bette's star being born in "the tubs." Bette and the Baths were a good match. From 1970 to 1972, Bette descended a rickety staircase and dazzled grown men in towels. She'd shake her breasts, appear in a turban à la Carmen Miranda, dance in ridiculous wedgies . . . nothing was too outrageous. Musically, she started as a torch singer, but her love for girl-group music, hubba-hubba, the blues, and Broadway

The Divine in a mad moment

would soon become her repertoire. Humor was added as Bette traded quips with the crowd, then began preparing jokes just for the fellas. And then there was the way the Divine Miss M spoke—like nobody else. The language, the way with the words, the turns of phrase, the musicality of her spiel would become key to her persona. It all worked—the clothes, the style, the songs, the shoes! From "Chattanooga Choo-Choo" to "Friends" to "Am I Blue?" to "Boogie Woogie Bugle Boy" . . . Bette Midler was evolving right before their eyes. The lessons learned in "the tubs" would shape Bette all her life.

Rex Reed in the *New York Daily News* was one of many who witnessed the creation of this new superstar: "Magic is in the air. Magic that removes the violence of the cold dark streets. The insecurities, the hates, the fears, the prejudices outside vanish in a haze of camp. It's Mary Martin asking if we believe in fairies. Yes. We do. Clap harder. And the Jewish Tinker Bell is right there in front of you. Twinkling, glittering, making soft musical chimes of peace. . . . That's what Bette Midler does to her audience. The boy clutches his towel and says, 'With Bette Midler, the world can overcome anything. Anything.' "

"Audiences just set me on fire," Bette once said. "When I go on the stage, it's like I'm at home throwing a party. I feel I can do any old thing." That was what the Baths gave Bette, and that sense of partying, that freedom to be eccentric, has carried through all her shows. The feeling of liberation and fun is what sets her concerts apart from all others.

Bette soon became too big for the Baths. The first major step up from the tubs was New Year's Eve at Philharmonic Hall at Lincoln Center. The *New York Times*'s Ian Dove hardly knew what to make of

Bette at the Palace *was the place to be in New York.*

her. He was reduced to explaining her act rather than critiquing it: "Miss Midler—now termed the Divine Miss M in her publicity—is perhaps better known for her camp re-creations of early rock 'n' roll songs, particularly those performed by female singing groups. . . . But to concentrate on this single aspect of Bette Midler, strong though it is, is to miss half the feast. She is quite capable of taking a contemporary ballad such as Leonard Russell's 'Superstar' and delivering it movingly with full respect for the content of the lyric. . . . She also uses the stage as if training for a track event. She bounds back and forth, barefoot or teetering on spike heels, calisthenically whirling her arms and developing a quick up-and-down squat to emphasize some point in a song. It proves that her muscle isn't only in her wide-ranging voice."

The sold-out Philharmonic engagement was proof that the word about Bette had spread. She was ready to move to the Great White Way, and there was no better Broadway spot than the Palace. The Palace, the same place the legendary Judy Garland had claimed as her own, was the first big-time concert stop for Bette Midler. After a year of touring the country, honing her act, learning her craft, Bette returned to New York, and in December 1973, *Bette Midler at the Palace* was the place to be.

Opening with an homage to Hawaii, her home, and singing her theme song, "Friends," Bette wasted no time in embracing the theater and making it her own. The first act was mostly jokes and songs—Nixon jokes interspersed with "Delta Dawn," a history lesson about the Palace, and a searing rendition of "I Shall Be Released." For the second-act opener, Bette appeared on stage atop a giant high-heel shoe! Picking up on the Harlettes' "Optimistic Voices" intro, Bette crooned "Lullaby of Broadway" as she descended the shoe. It was spectacle and glitz, it was funny and wild, it was inventive and brilliant. It then segued into "Boogie Woogie Bugle Boy." "Do You Want to Dance?," "Surabaya Johnny," "Hello in There," and "Higher and Higher" followed. With "The Chapel of Love," another sight appeared on stage—a huge heart with the words of the song. When she implored her "friends" to sing along, the Palace became a love-in. When Bette Midler landed on the cover of *Newsweek* soon after the opening at the Palace, no one was too surprised. She was the toast of

"Stay With Me" became a Bette showstopper. (Michael Gillespie Collection)

the town. And when *Bette Midler at the Palace* won a special Tony—for Best Special Performance on Broadway—it was just desserts. The lady had earned the acclaim.

For many stars, a show that successful would have been the pinnacle. How can you top a big, splashy, Tony Award–winning extravaganza? In Bette Midler's case, you create another brilliant

show. *Clams on the Half-Shell Revue* was just that kind of production, but more scripted and Broadway-oriented than the Palace show. After Bette's meeting with writer Bruce Vilanch and hiring director Joe Layton, *Clams* took shape. It would not be a rehash of *the Palace* show; it would be something special. It included a guest star, musician Lionel Hampton, whose very presence added class to the proceedings. Layton's contributions were immeasurable. A brilliant musical director and musical stager, Layton had shaped Barbra Streisand's classic one-woman shows for CBS-TV.

For Bette, Layton was a fount of invention, beginning with the opening number, which spoofed Broadway itself. Bette appeared on stage lying in the bed of a giant clam. As the clam opened, she rose in sequins to sing "Oklahoma." The oddity of it all was charming. Layton also conceived a true showstopper for *Clams*. As a first-act closer, Bette appeared in the palm of a life-sized King Kong. Images like the clam and the giant ape were impressive and stunning. When *Clams* opened at the Minskoff Theater, April 14, 1975, the audiences were dazzled. However, it seemed some Broadway critics were not. In the *New York Times*, Clive Barnes complained, "She uses the theater as if it were a nightclub, and plays with the audience as if it were a shoal of fish. Her rapport is extraordinary, and she can laugh and insult, and laugh again. But what has happened to Miss Midler in this show? Oh, of course, enough of her comes through to keep the fans whirring, but something has happened. The vulgarity has become glossy rather than tatty." Yet even Barnes had to concede, "For all this, when everything is done, by heck, New York is still her town and she is still its best Bette."

Bette set records at Radio City—thirty sold-out shows!

Despite the popularity of the show and the financial success,

Bette found the experience wanting. Because the show was structured so much like a Broadway musical, there was no room for improvisation. As Bette complained after *Clams* ended, "The trouble with the *Clams* show was there was no room for spontaneity. . . . There was no room for me. I dealt with my lines and my costumes and my songs in that show. I was amazingly *professional*. And it was a fabulous show. But I had become separated from that character. And that depressed me."

Bette toured with a portable, scaled-down version of *Clams,* called *the Depression Tour* (named for her third album, *Songs for the New Depression*). King Kong was still part of the act, but other elements were dropped to accommodate the traveling. Added to the show was an ingenious new character, Vicki Eydie, the ultimate bad lounge act. The reworked show also gave Bette plenty of room to be spontaneous, and that was the show that was preserved for posterity: it was videotaped as *The Fabulous Bette Midler* for HBO and committed to vinyl as *Live at Last.*

In 1977, Bette conceived another kind of show, one that would bring her closer to the audience and out of the big arenas. She wanted to do a more intimate program. Indeed, it was called *An Intimate Evening with Bette Midler* (a.k.a. *the Club Tour*), and it was booked into nightclubs around the country, usually those seating around six hundred people. What the show lacked in spectacle, it made up for in humor. Bette was in rare form, opening most shows with the line, "I stand before you nipples to the wind!" Topicality was key, and Bette wrote (or had written for her) material for each city. She talked about her music, asking fans to move her albums to the rock section of record stores if they ever found them in the "female vocalist" bin next to the likes of Vicki Carr and Shirley Bassey. "Oh, please! The last thing I want in this life is to rot next to Liza Minnelli!" Musically, Bette's show was as eclectic as ever: "In the Mood," "Empty Bed Blues," "La Vie en Rose," "Superstar," "Leader of the Pack," "Doctor Long John."

The Fabulous Bette Midler *was the HBO special version of* **the Depression Tour.**

175

As for spontaneity, there was more than enough room for it. In one show at the Paradise in Boston, when she was given a glass slipper by a member of the audience, Bette thanked the person by singing a completely impromptu—and incredibly charming—rendition of "Someday My Prince Will Come" (from *Snow White and the Seven Dwarfs*).

When Bette played the Copacabana in New York, January 12, 1978, the critics embraced her. Even the usually curmudgeonly Arthur Bell in the *Village Voice* was charmed: "She is sensational when she torches. 'Drinking Again' is a Sinatra-type song, the lament of a very sad lady, and Bette's rendition makes clear that she is an actress as well as a chanteuse and a clown." On the other hand, John S. Wilson in the *New York Times* was more impressed with Bette's comedy: "Miss Midler launched into an energetic hour and a half of sharp, pungent one-liners and fervent songs. Initially treading the lines of bawdiness somewhat gingerly, she was soon sloshing joyously across them with an earthy wit that kept her audience rising to point after point, building up to a series of what she calls her 'Sophie Tucker' stories. . . . She sustains the flow of her barbs and quips with a humor that turns on her as much as it does on other subjects."

Following the Club Tour, Bette had two major projects in store: her first network primetime TV special, *Ol' Red Hair Is Back;* and filming her first motion picture, *The Rose*. Then, in September 1978, Bette commenced her first world tour. Documented in her comic memoir, *A View From a Broad*, the tour would eventually

*The **Clams** show was more scripted and structured. (Michael Gillespie Collection)*

become *Bette Midler: Divine Madness!* Staged by Bette and Jerry Blatt, and written by Bette, Jerry, and Bruce Vilanch, *Divine Madness* played some U.S. dates before settling into an extended run at Broadway's Majestic Theater, December 5, 1979. The Staggering Harlettes— Franny Eisenberg, Linda Hart, Paulette McWilliams—were there, as was break-dancer Shabba-Doo. The most significant creation in *Divine Madness* was Delores DeLago, the mermaid who aspires to be a great performer. Without feet, Delores nevertheless "dances" thanks to her motorized wheelchair. The character was an outgrowth of Vicki Eydie, the main difference being that Delores had fins, not feet. The inclusion of Delores also gave Bette a chance to add ball-twirling to the show. Like a true vaudevillian, Bette gave her audience a little bit of everything!

The New York critics loved Bette personally, but her show received mixed notices. *New York Post* reviewer Ira Mayer wrote: "Bette Midler remains a brilliant stage performer—one so good that she can boost subpar material to acceptable standards and, when the song is right, be chillingly dramatic. . . . As always, Bette was the main attraction. And nothing—not even songs that are pointless for her— could obscure just how talented she is." Robert Palmer in the *New York Times* concurred: "Like Delores DeLago, who makes an appearance near the end of the first act, Miss Midler has lots of lung power and an underwhelming amount of taste. . . . Miss Midler is such a pro at faking emotions that it's difficult for this listener, at least, to catch much feeling from her singing, even when she seems to mean it. Ultimately, the show's implicit message—pop culture as trash—is its dominant message. It sparkles to hide its emptiness." *Divine Madness* wound up as Bette's first—and only—concert film. Filmed under less than optimal conditions, it still stands as a powerful example of her artistry.

Bette needed time—and took time—away from the stage to recharge her batteries. She worked on other projects, most notably *Jinxed,* the problematic comedy she made after the *Divine Madness* movie.

By 1982, stung by the criticism from *Jinxed* and anxious to get

The **Clams on the Half-Shell Revue** *was a big Broadway hit. (Playbill)*

back to the world she knew best—concerts—Bette planned a new show. Influenced by New Wave music—which would also show in her next album, *No Frills*—Bette conceived a very different kind of tour: *De Tour*. There would be less nostalgia—no hubba-hubba, no platform shoes—and an emphasis on art. Of course, it wasn't all "artsy-fartsy," as Bette would say. Delores DeLago was back with her wheelchair, and Bette sang "Pretty Legs and Great Big Knockers" while holding oversized balloons that looked like a pair of breasts. And there were plenty of Soph jokes, too.

The tour traveled to nineteen cities across America, and it was a difficult tour. In one stop outside Detroit—Clarkston, Michigan—Bette crumbled. As she told interviewers after the fact, "It was 140 degrees. I hadn't been sleeping, and I felt sick as a dog before the show. During the number 'Pretty Legs and Great Big Knockers,' I felt ready to faint. I ran off stage for the balloons I needed for the number and I blacked out. One lonely little balloon came bouncing back on stage with no Bette behind it. . . . I was sure I wouldn't get better. I felt panic-stricken and I couldn't stop crying. Then I started to take stock. I thought of all the people I hadn't seen. And I really wanted to see my mother, but I couldn't." It turned out that Bette was suffering from heat exhaustion and a gastrointestinal ailment. After she recovered, she finished *De Tour,* then filmed it as an HBO TV special, calling it *Bette Midler: Art or Bust!*

A decade would pass before Bette reclaimed the title of world's greatest concert performer. In the interim, she got married, had a baby, had two monster hit singles, became a major movie star, and generally lived a full life. Occasionally, she flirted with the idea of touring, but with her daughter, Sophie, still in elementary school, Bette was reluctant to leave her while she went out on the road.

By 1993, things had changed; Bette (and Sophie) could accommodate a tour. All Bette's experiences would shape her triumphant return to the stage, *Experience the Divine*. More than ego or convenience was behind Bette's comeback. After putting her heart

An early incarnation of Delores DeLago at Radio City, 1983. (Michael Gillespie Collection)

and soul, blood, sweat, and tears into the
production of *For the Boys,* only to have the
film fail at the box office, Bette was disen-
chanted with Hollywood. On stage, she
could be in charge. As she told the *Boston
Globe*'s Steve Morse: "I had a variety of
motivations for going back on tour. I miss
the crowds. I miss the reaction. And I miss
doing my own work. I mean, whatever it is,
it is my own and I don't have to answer to
anybody else for it. For the last ten years,
I've been saying yes to other people and
having to do what they want and it's been
exhausting. Enough already. . . . I'm a
show person. I love to do shows. I love the
idea of turning the lights on something
and turning it into something magical or

beautiful. . . . I like to be close and hear the audience laugh. That's a
major part of what I do—and to have some sort of roller coaster
where they get to experience a lot of things, not just one thing. It's
like therapy in a way. You get to laugh; you cry once or twice; and
you think about things, though not too deeply." That's exactly what
Experience the Divine delivered.

On September 14, at New York's Radio City Music Hall, Bette
descended from the ceiling in a golden swing to the fanfare of trum-
pets, singing "Friends." *Experience the Divine* was truly a celebration of
Bette Midler. The show reviewed her twenty-five-year career and commented on it. She sang a rap song called "I Look Good!" and no one
who saw her would dare disagree; she looked great. There was a
salute to burlesque, topped by Bette's soaring "Rose's Turn" from
Gypsy. The burlesque section also was the perfect spot for her Soph
jokes. Delores DeLago oiled up her wheelchair and returned for an
extended piece that spoofed infomercials. "Ukelele Lady" was a bow
to Hawaii. And, naturally, there were the inspirational ballads ("Have
I sung the ballad yet? Was it wonderful?")—"The Rose," "From a
Distance," and "Wind Beneath My Wings." She topped it all with
"The Glory of Love."

Bette took her family on tour with her and discovered that
singing and dancing was in the genes. Sophie was fascinated by the
process. Bette even let her be in it: "I put her in 'Ukelele Lady.' She

Some business from **De
Tour**—*Bette and a giant boob
(Michael Gillespie Collection)*

sits and plunks her ukelele and sings a song and has a pretty wonderful time. She loves slapping that makeup on. We call it going to 'burlesque camp.' She loves the trappings, the feather boas, the makeup and the hairdos. She loves the costumes and the sets. She's a great kid and she's been a great sport."

The critics were nearly unanimous in their praise. "Yes, Miss M is still divine," Robert Hilburn of the *Los Angeles Times* wrote. "Returning to concerts after a ten-year break, the preeminent mainstream pop performer of the seventies and early eighties could have wowed us simply with a recycled greatest-hits package. And Bette Midler did employ many of her old standbys Wednesday at the Universal Amphitheatre, including familiar record hits, ribald Sophie Tucker–style jokes and tacky Delores DeLago's lounge act spectacle. What made the evening so triumphant, however, was Midler's undiminished daring and vision. . . . Midler said goodnight with 'The Glory of Love,' with its classic refrain about how in life you win a little, lose a little. In some ways, the selection seemed almost too neat a summary of the evening's uplifting message. But she sang the song with such warmth and heart that even it came out a winner. On this night, it was yet another example of the glory of Bette."

Experience the Divine toured in 1993 and returned for more dates in 1994. In 1996, Bette revamped the show—adding references to her smash-hit movie *The First Wives Club*—and put it on tape for an HBO special. The show—*Diva Las Vegas*—aired January 18, 1997, to glorious reviews.

Once upon a time, Bette said of her performing, "I have pretty good instincts. I go right to the line and even if I do things in bad taste, I do them in such a way that it's okay. I've thought about just going out and performing straight. Sometimes I wonder about that. But everybody else does that and it's so boring." "Boring" is a

*"Everyone's Gone to the Moon"—***De Tour*** (Michael Gillespie Collection)*

word that could never apply to Bette Midler. The best of Bette has always been on stage, from the little girl who would sing "Lullaby of Broadway" to the accomplished superstar warbling "The Glory of Love." Midler on stage is sheer magic, and that is truly her most divine legacy.

ONE MORE ROUND:
THE LATEST, GREATEST BETTE,
DIVA LAS VEGAS

On January 10, 1997, fifty-two-year-old Bette Midler returned to the stage once again. The occasion was the filming of her updated *Experience the Divine* show, renamed *Diva Las Vegas*. The show that played the MGM Grand Garden was a spectacle, a monumental concert by a monumental concert artist. Entertainment journalist and longtime Bette Midler fan Todd Sussman was fortunate enough to see *Diva Las Vegas* live. His in-depth review of the show offers insights into the magic of Midler live and at her very best. As you will read, he thought she was simply divine:

> The Divine Miss M. Mega movie star. Showstopping singer. Oscar-worthy actress. All Girl and even more woman. Waitress at the banquet of life. Queen of Compost. The Bette-meister. Bette-o-rama. One of the first—and last—true superstars. Bette Midler fits all of these descriptions . . . and in her Las Vegas concert, they all come into play. One moment, she's mesmerizing an audience with the way she sells a song. The next, she's causing a laugh riot. If there's one thing this show woman knows, it's how to put on a great show.

> Here we have *Diva Las Vegas*, live at the MGM Grand. The arena has, indeed, been very good in delivering top talent to its patrons. The last time I was there was to see that other superstar whose name also starts with *B* . . . Barbra Streisand. But that's a whole 'nother story. This night was all about Bette.

> Miss Midler really lived up to her Divine billing, even before she descended from her cut-out clouds and landed onto center stage. On the day of the show, Friday, January 10, the MGM Grand Hotel was decked out in Midler imagery. Posters for the event were prominently displayed. They featured a stunning photograph of Bette in a gold sequined gown, sprawled

Back after ten years, Bette was hilarious and riveting in the **Experience the Divine** *tour. (Michael Gillespie Collection)*

out on a bed of red poker chips. What a wonderful way to say "Vegas," or as Midler puts it, "Oy Vegas!" The image was omnipresent: bigger than life on the gargantuan MGM marquee, showcased in the labyrinth of casino rooms, and even bolted into the hotel's elevators. Alas, the poster was something of a teaser; it was for promotional use only, not for sale to the diehard fans who just had to have one. Luckily, Bette herself was more accessible in a sense, giving her audience exactly what it came to see: the flash and the trash, the glitter and the glitz, the mermaids and the music. So on with the show.

Midler's concert was tailor-made for her—and us. After a snippet of her very first theme song, "Friends," she segued into a rap song appropriately titled "I Look Good." This was pure poetry in motion, literally. In form-fitting black stagewear, complemented by high-heel pumps with wrap-around ankle straps, the newly svelte Bette walked the walk (you know, the famous one we've come to know and love in movies like *Down and Out in Beverly Hills* and *Outrageous Fortune*) and talked the talk. Hearing Bette proclaim "I Look Good" made me recall Barbra Streisand proclaiming "I'm Still Here," the specialty song Barbra used in her Vegas concert to cover the trials and tribulations of a legend who defied her detractors and remained on top. Now it was Bette's turn to review history. And just look at what Midler had to go through to look so good—albeit, to survive—as the lyrics indicate: *'Boys and girls, I have done it all/I've been compromised, Walt Disney-ized/Dried out, detoxed and Jurrasified/Macroed, microed, lipoed/And psychoanalyzed.'*

No wonder this diva has our respect! She has earned her stripes. And more importantly, that night, she was willing to earn them all over again. She was energized for this rapper's delight, giving her backup singers, the Harlettes, a run for their money.

As a nice touch, she turned the tables to acknowledge her viewers, a diverse crowd peppered with high rollers in their finest velvet garb, some former movie costars (James Caan, Lainie Kazan), Nevada locals, out-of-towners, and the loyal fans in the front row. Midler hilariously referred to those up front as "the American Express Gold Card ticket holders . . . yuppie swine!" Act One provided a musical journey through many Midlerian song styles. She did the trademark sultry standard (every diva used to do at least one per LP, some built entire LPs out of them). In this case, it was "Spring Can Really Hang You Up the Most." The lush arrangement, combined with Bette's shimmering vocals, gave new life to this chestnut. The song also gave her the chance to show off her incredible range, hitting the highs as well as the lows. She was, all at once, breathtaking and heartbreaking, and this wasn't even one of those "inspirational ballads," a term Midler used to refer to her smash-hit theme songs—"The Rose," "From a Distance," and "The Wind Beneath My Wings." With "Spring," Midler showed that she doesn't need all the pomp and circumstance in order to really shine.

Of course, all the musical frills were still offered. We got the retro big-band singer harmonies of "Miss Otis Regrets." Another crowd pleaser. We got the now-obligatory (to Midler tours) disco medley. Included here was her reading of "Rock the Boat," which, though very brief, still qualifies as time capsule–quality camp. We got the Broadway-to-TV belters, as in "Rose's Turn" from *Gypsy*. (How dare they not give her the Emmy for that!) And we got a mini–burlesque show with a song from the vaults, "Pretty Legs and Great Big Knockers," excavated from *De Tour*, her 1983 road show. "Pretty Legs" was interwoven with a slew of Soph jokes. This was fitting for a performer known for transcending the boundaries of good taste, long before Madonna removed her training bra, or any of her bras, for that matter.

The most magical moments from the first half of her concert, however, came when Midler brought us back to the movies . . . *her* movies . . . namely, *The First Wives Club* and *The Rose*. To start, Midler paid ample tribute to *First Wives*, with parody lyrics to "Everything's Coming Up Roses" (changing "Roses" to "Grosses"), at

"Have I sung the ballad yet? Was it wonderful?" (Michael Gillespie Collection)

which point Midler basked in the film's through-the-roof box office ticket sales ("I'm in a hit, a big f***ing hit, baby!"), as well as a soaring solo version of "You Don't Own Me," which Midler had originally performed in the movie with her costars, Goldie Hawn and Diane Keaton. "The Rose," of course, became the evening's first inspirational ballad, and after all these years (eighteen, to be precise), her interpretation is still new and exciting. Many audience members returned the love that was channeled through this number by holding up red, silk, glow-in-the-dark roses and swaying them to the music. It was a one-time-only moment, containing all the spontaneity and electricity which characterize the experience of seeing a show live. Not even the HBO cameras could capture that moment, which invisibly linked every member of the audience.

In Act Two, Midler lugged out some perennial favorites: Delores DeLago on wheels, balls on a string, early hit singles such as "Boogie Woogie Bugle Boy" and "Do You Want to Dance?," and, to close the show, her most recent chart-toppers, which have become her latest theme songs. The Delores section was rooted in America's fleeting preoccupation with infomercials, New Age self-help gurus, and twelve-step programs. Admittedly, this material, which was culled from Bette's *Experience the Divine* tour from 1993, seemed somewhat dated. And yet, Midler managed to get mucho mileage out of it. She was absolutely radiant. Undeniably, the audience still cherished the sight of Midler as a mermaid in a wheelchair doing her New Age shtick, and they rewarded her with a standing ovation.

Nevertheless, Bette definitely saved the best for last. This was the concert within the concert, the singer standing in front of the microphone in a sexy, low-cut sequined auburn dress, simply and elegantly singing her signature songs, including "From a Distance" and "The Wind Beneath My Wings," along with a jazzed-up version of "To Comfort You" from her most recent CD, *Bette of Roses*. More than once, these songs brought the audience to its feet, especially her rendition of "Stay With Me" from *The Rose*. With that song, every emotion registering on Midler's face rang true, and her voice met the challenge of the musical peaks and valleys, the almost primal screams incorporated into this tale of abandonment and rejection, the ultimate victim song. She truly has to *work* this song when-

ever she sings it . . . and work it she did. This is why
she gets the big bucks, and why she deserves them.
This is why her devotees will pay to see her concerts
more than once, flying halfway around the globe if
they have to. On stage, Bette Midler remains one of
the most compelling performers of her generation,
and on that Friday night in Las Vegas, she surpassed
my greatest expectations.

Rehearsing for a show

NINE

specially Bette:
The Television Specials

The Fabulous Bette Midler
JUNE 19, 1976, HBO

The Fabulous Bette Midler was Bette's first concert filmed for television, in particular, pay TV. HBO broadcast the two-hour-twenty-minute stage show, taped lived on February 7 and 8 in Cleveland, in its entirety, without censoring any of Bette's ribald humor. This is truly a time capsule performance, and in every way it's superb. The program is essentially the *Depression Tour,* which was a road show version of *Clams on the Half-Shell,* and when released for home video, the special was renamed *The Bette Midler Show.*

"In the end, she wins, or at least overwhelms. I stayed with Miss Midler and was glad I did. Her incredible dress of ruffles out of Polly Peachum by way of *The Threepenny Opera,* her imitation of Shelley Winters in *The Poseidon Adventure,* her Sophie Tucker routines, her entrance stretched across the palm of a giant King Kong, her routines with a superb three-woman supporting group—whatever the faults or reservations, the result added up to remarkable television."—John J. O'Connor, *New York Times*

"Hello in There" was all the more poignant with Emmett Kelly.

Bette Midler: Ol' Red Hair Is Back

DECEMBER 7, 1977, NBC
(With Dustin Hoffman and Emmett Kelly)

They said it couldn't be done: saucy, sassy, wild Bette Midler on network television?! In primetime? NBC took a chance, secure that the extraordinary talent of Bette Midler could be harnessed into a spectacular hour of television. And that's exactly what *Ol' Red Hair Is Back* was, Bette Midler carefully and lovingly presented for folks sitting on their couches in American living rooms coast to coast. Of course, this wasn't Bette's first experience in primetime: she had guested on specials for Cher (with Elton John and Flip Wilson), Burt Bacharach (doing "Boogie Woogie Bugle Boy" in three-part split-screen, as well as "Superstar"), Bing Crosby (singing with Bing and the Mills Brothers), and even Neil Sedaka (doing a duet on "Love Will Keep Us Together"). Network audiences were also familiar with Bette from her numerous appearances on *The Tonight Show With Johnny Carson*. But—with the exception of the relatively small audience that had been able to see the HBO special (in 1976 only about 10 percent of the country had the cable outlet)—not many people had ever seen a full hour of Bette Midler. What they saw was a revelation—funny, vulnerable, lovable, playful, silly, serious, coy, flirty . . . Bette revealed a plethora of emotions in comedy, sketches, and especially in song.

Ol' Red Hair Is Back *began with the* **Clams** *opening.*

Directed and produced by Dwight Hemion and Gary Smith, the pair who had created magical TV specials for Barbra Streisand (*Color Me Barbra*) and Frank Sinatra (*A Man and His Music*), among others, brought their considerable skills to the Midler project. Wisely, they borrowed bits from Bette on stage—notably the *Clams* opening—and placed Bette front and center before a live audience, with a runway to walk out into the crowd. For guests,

the Midler project. Wisely, they borrowed bits from Bette on stage—notably the *Clams* opening—and placed Bette front and center before a live audience, with a runway to walk out into the crowd. For guests,

188

Bette had the great clown Emmett Kelly, who provided a poignant, silent counterpoint to Bette's soulful rendition of "Hello in There." The other guest was Dustin Hoffman, an actor you would never expect to see on a musical variety special. Somehow, though, the incongruity worked, and Hoffman was surprisingly charming in his sequence. But overall, the magic was Midler. The show won Bette an Emmy when it was named outstanding variety special. Why NBC (or another network) did not get Bette to do a follow-up is still a mystery.

"Carving out her distinctive niche between the kooky vulnerability of Barbra Streisand and the calculated 'red-hot mama' brassiness of Sophie Tucker, Miss Midler becomes a human projectile of almost irresistible energy."—John J. O'Connor, *New York Times*

Bette Midler: Art or Bust!

AUGUST 20, 1984, HBO

Bette Midler: Art or Bust! was something different for Bette. It was a mixture of a concert—her *De Tour* show—and a TV special. Director Thomas Schlamme jazzed up the proceedings with animation, special effects, and graphics that elevated the material from the traditional concert special. Interestingly, the material from her *No Frills* album inspired Bette to try new things. There are still touches of the familiar—in particular, Delores DeLago in her motorized wheelchair with her three sisters—as well as a beautiful rendition of "The Rose" over the end credits, but as presented in *Art or Bust!,* it was all fresh and original.

Delores DeLago, the toast of Chicago, starred in **Art or Bust!**

Bette Midler: Art or Bust! was filmed in the Northrup Auditorium at the University of Minnesota and broadcast on HBO

August 20, 1984. When it was released on home video, two "extras" were inserted into the program. The first is a flashback of Bette at the Continental Baths circa 1971—in grainy black and white—making an entrance à la Carmen Miranda (singing "Marihauna"), then flopping around in a halter top while singing a hubba-hubba rendition of "Chattanooga Choo-Choo." The other archive clip is Bette performing at a 1973 United Jewish Appeal telethon, offering to drop her dress for Israel. When someone meets her challenge—offering a $5,000 pledge—Bette peels off her gown to reveal a sexy slip.

"Bette Midler takes risks that other performers do not. She attempts to be touching, bawdy, and funny, often simultaneously. When she succeeds she is brilliant, and when she fails she is done in

Mondo Beyondo **was not** **enough Bette. (HBO)**

by her own excess. On *Bette Midler: Art or Bust!* she succeeds more often than she fails; she is, in fact, close to being an absolute winner, and if she were an Olympic gymnast, going for a perfect 10, she would get a 9.9."—John Corry, *New York Times*

Bette Midler's Mondo Beyondo

MARCH 19, 1988, HBO

(WITH BILL IRWIN, PAUL ZALOOM, AND THE KIPPER KIDS—Martin von Haselberg and Brian Routh)

You know those weird, wacky and often bizarre public access TV shows? You know, the ones that are so cheesy and tacky that they're actually funny? Well, if you do, you'll probably get what Bette was spoofing with *Mondo Beyondo.* If you haven't, *Mondo Beyondo* will leave you scratching your head. One of the funniest things in the special is Bette's Mondo character, a red-haired, busty Italian diva who searches the globe to bring viewers "cutting edge" entertainment. Created by Bette and collaborator Jerry Blatt, Mondo is the only redeeming feature in this strained pseudo-special.

The acts Mondo presents are of varied talents—the opening featurette, Yes/No People, looking like a precursor to the hit show *Stomp;* Bill Irwin doing sophisticated mime and dance; Paul Zaloom cavorting in a garbage dump; Bette as Eudora P. Quickly singing a Jeanette MacDonald favorite; and the Kipper Kids (in a real lowlight) splattering each other with Spaghetti-Os, eggs, flour, and shaving cream!

"Bette Midler is hilarious. The show is the best spoof of the TV variety format. . . . Midler is making fun of the public access show, one of those wonderfully tacky vanity cable programs. Midler as Mondo Beyondo—a character created by Jerry Blatt and Midler—continues demonstrating she is one of the most outrageous funny people on TV, a maximalist comedienne in a minimalist age." —Marvin Kitman, *Newsday*

Diva Las Vegas *brought Bette back to HBO.*

Diva Las Vegas

JANUARY 18, 1997, HBO

"From a Distance" was an emotional high from **Diva**. *(Michael Gillespie Collection)*

Ten years passed between Bette's 1983 *De Tour* and the *Experience the Divine* tour. And it was another four years before home viewers got a chance to see an older, wiser, and just as dynamic Bette Midler in concert. *Experience the Divine* came to TV as *Diva Las Vegas*, shot in two nights—January 10 and 11—at the MGM Grand Garden in Las Vegas. Everything about *Diva Las Vegas* was big, brassy, timely, and, in many ways, a culmination of all that Bette Midler had been doing for nearly twenty-five years in the public eye.

Beginning with her signature song, "Friends," *Diva Las Vegas* celebrated Bette. Her rap parody, "I Look Good," was as funny as it was self-congratulatory. In fact, Bette did look good—strutting her stuff after so many years, singing better than ever, joking and kidding about herself and the world around her. It was clear that the magic Bette Midler first displayed at the Continental Baths and the Palace was still intact. *Diva Las Vegas* also featured a salute to burlesque—topped by Bette's bravura performance of "Rose's Turn" from *Gypsy*—Delores DeLago and a chorus of six motorized wheelchairs, a retinue of Soph jokes, and Bette's very successful "inspirational ballads": "From a Distance," "Wind Beneath My Wings," "The Rose." In many ways, *Diva Las Vegas* was Bette Midler's greatest hits, only it wasn't restricted to music.

"A dazzling tour de force of monumental proportions! And that was just the first fifteen minutes! *Diva Las Vegas,* Midler's latest TV special, proved indisputably that there's plenty of life in the old girl yet. We should all have as much. Midler was in great voice, great face, and great form. The balance of new material and old standbys seemed ideal, as did the ratio of music to comedy. . . . Producer-direc-

tor Marty Callner did everybody a favor by concentrating his cameras
on the stage and the star and not, as so many directors of live concerts do, on people in the audience. Who wants to see people in the
audience? There was a stunning overhead shot of Midler as she
reclined near the piano singing "Spring Can Really Hang You Up the
Most" and plenty of other excellent camera work. . . . At its best
moments, her voice has a warmth that is lovely and enveloping. She's
a wonder at achieving what might be called Bombastic Intimacy. One
assumes the concert will be made available later on video, but for
now it remains another resounding triumph for HBO as well as, of
course, for Miss M."—Tom Shales, *Washington Post*

The burlesque section of **Diva**
included Bette's homage to
Gypsy. *(Michael Gillespie*
Collection)

*Soph jokes are a
staple of every Bette
Midler concert.*

TEN

Jokes From a Broad

One of the keys to the success of Bette Midler is her incredible sense of humor. It's part of her persona, part of the image that she has projected since she first stood in the spotlight to perform. Whether reeling off Soph jokes, doing her impression of Shelley Winters in *The Poseidon Adventure* ("The P Adventure!"), or teetering on heels as she ambles back and forth on the concert stage, Bette Midler has always been a very funny lady.

Perhaps the most concrete example of Midler's humor is found in the pages of the two books she's penned—*A View From a Broad* (1978, Simon and Schuster) and *The Saga of Baby Divine* (Crown, 1983). *A View From a Broad* is Bette's fanciful, primarily fictional, account of her first world concert tour. As Bette herself said, "It's jaunty. Some of it is absolutely real and some of it is totally off the wall, but that's the way my life is, you know? It's up to the reader to tread this sodden, marshy fen and come up with some kind of conclusion, if he's interested, about my life."

The Saga of Baby Divine is a lovingly adorable children's book about a little girl who can only say one word—"More." Beautifully illustrated by Todd Schorr, with rhyming verse by Bette, it's not too hard to get the message in this fairy tale, and to appreciate Bette's wry humor. And any similarities between Baby Divine and Bette

Midler are on purpose!

As a comedienne, Bette has shone in films, in TV appearances, and most especially in concert. One of the hallmarks of every Midler concert is the Soph jokes. Written by Jerry Blatt, Bruce Vilanch, Bette, and others over the years, the Soph jokes have become legendary. Collected here are some of the most memorable.

———————

"You know, my girlfriend Clementine is a filthy, vulgar old broad—much like myself. She likes to keep me abreast of all the filthy rotten jokes and filthy rotten songs. The other day, she rang me up and said, 'Soph, listen to this one. You never heard anything like it. What do you get when you cross a donkey with an onion?' I said, 'Clementine, I have no idea. What the hell do you get when you cross a donkey with an onion?' 'Well, usually you get an onion with very long ears, but occasionally, when the stars are just right, you get a piece of ass that's so wonderful it makes you want to cry!' "

———————

Ernie: Soph, did you just fart?
Sophie: Of course I did! Ya think I always smell like this?!

———————

"I will never forget it! I was in the woods with my boyfriend Ernie and he said to me, 'Soph? These woods sure are dark. I sure wish I had a flashlight.' I said to him, 'So do I, Ernie. You've been munching grass for the last ten minutes!"

———————

"I will never forget it, ya know. It was the first time I met my boyfriend Ernie. I was in my underground parking garage, down Miami Beach way, when this beautiful black Mercedes pulled into the garage and parked. I strolled on over to the car. I said, 'My, my, my, my, my. This is the most beautiful car I've ever seen.' Ernie said, 'Do you think so?' I said, 'Yes, and I think you're the handsomest man I've ever seen.' Ernie said, 'Do you think so?' I said, 'Yes, and a handsome face deserves a little kiss' . . . and I gave him one. (*smack*) I said, 'A handsome tush deserves a little squeeze' . . . and I gave him one. (*squeeze*) Then, I issued the coup de grace. I said, 'I bet you're something in the equipment department.' He said, 'Many HAVE written home to say

Bette's memoir of her world tour was a bestseller.

so.' I said, 'I'd love to see it.' He said, 'Would you?' I said, 'Yes.' He unzipped his fly and there it was! Long story short, I held it in my hand. I said (*viciously slapping the hand holding 'it' with each word*), 'DON'T YOU EVER PARK IN MY SPACE AGAIN!!' "

"I will never forget it, you know . . . for the longest time I didn't wear no underwear. I used to drive my boyfriend Ernie absolutely batty. . . . One day, I caught a terrible cold. Ernie says to me, 'Soph, you've got a terrible cold, you've got to go see the doctor right away.' I says , 'All right, Ernie, make an appointment for me.' So he rang up the doctor, and this is what he said, unbeknownst to me, 'Doc, I'm sending Soph over; she's got a terrible cold. But that's not the problem. The problem is she don't wear no underwear. Tell her the reason she's got this cold is on account of she don't wear no underwear. Ya got that?' 'Right-o!' says the doc. So I, like a schmuck, trot on down to the doctor's office. Doctor says, 'Open your mouth and say ah.' I opened my mouth and said ah. The doc looked down my throat. He said, 'Soph, you ain't wearin' no underwear.' I said, 'I beg your pardon, Doctor!?' He says, 'Soph, you ain't wearin' no underwear.' I said, 'Doctor, you can look down my throat and see I ain't wearin' no underwear?' He said, 'That's right, Soph.' I said, 'Doc, do me a favor? Look up my ass and tell me if my hat's on straight!' "

"I came home from work the other day and my boyfriend Ernie said to me, 'Soph . . . ya know, if you learned to cook we could fire the chef.' I said to him, 'Ernie, if you learned to fuck, we could fire the chauffeur!' "

"I will never forget it, you know, I came home one day and found my ninety-year-old boyfriend Ernie making love to another woman on the living room sofa. I became so enraged that I picked Ernie up and threw him out the window—down ten stories, killing the poor old son of a bitch. Two months later when I was on trial for murder, the judge said to me, 'Soph, we all know how much you loved Ernie. What would make you throw him out the window?' I looked at him and said, 'Your Honor, at ninety years of age, I figured that if he could fuck, he could fly!' "

"I will never forget it! It was on the occasion of Ernie's eightieth birthday. He rang me up and said, 'Soph, Soph! I just married me a twenty-year-old girl. What do you think of that?' I said to him, 'Ernie, when I

The Saga of Baby Divine *was a divine children's book.*

am eighty, I shall marry me a twenty-year-old boy. And let me tell you something, Ernie: Twenty goes into eighty a lot more than eighty goes into twenty!"

"Oh, I will never forget it! It was on the occasion of my eightieth birthday. My boyfriend Ernie bought for me a tombstone, and on that tombstone he had inscribed: HERE LIES SOPH—COLD AS USUAL. Not being one to take that kind of thing lying down, I went out and bought Ernie a tombstone, and on that tombstone, I had inscribed: HERE LIES ERNIE—STIFF AT LAST!"

"I will never forget it, you know, my girlfriend Clementine and I were having tea one day when the doorbell rang. It was the delivery boy with a box of flowers. I opened them and inside were a dozen long-stem roses with a note that said, 'All my love, Ernie.' I said to Clementine, 'You know what this means. . . . Now I'm going to have to spend the next two weeks lying flat on my back with my legs spread wide open.' Clementine looked at me and said, 'What's the matter, Soph? Don't you have a vase?'"

"I was hanging out my laundry just the other day, and my girlfriend Clementine leaned over the fence and said, 'Soph, how is it that you can hang out your laundry and don't get caught in the rain like the rest of us girls do?' I said to her, 'Clementine, it is a simple proposition. I wake up in the morning, roll over, and take a good look at my boyfriend Ernie. If it's layin' on the left, I know it's gonna be a sunny day. If it's layin' on the right, I know it's gonna rain.' Clementine says to me, 'Soph, s'pose it's standin' straight up in the middle?' I said to her, 'Clementine, you idiot . . . who the hell wants to do laundry on a day like that anyway?!'"

"I will never forget it, ya know. I was in bed last night with my boyfriend Ernie. And he said to me, 'Soph, you got no tits and a tight box.' I said to him, 'Ernie, get off my back!'"

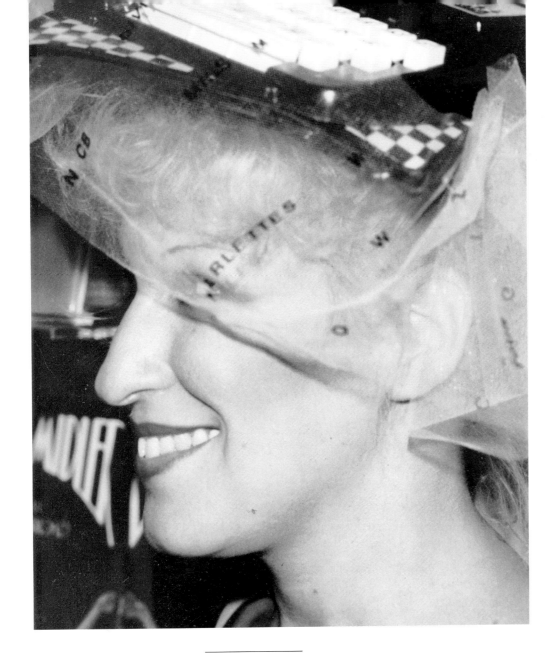

"I will never forget it, you know, it was my birthday and in honor of my birthday my boyfriend Ernie told me that he'd do anything to please me. I told him to kiss me where it smells. So he took me to New Jersey!"

"I will never forget it, ya know? It was just after my boyfriend Ernie, Lucky Ernie—World War I flying ace—came home from that very same war. Ah, what a war it was! He took me up to his apartment. He stripped me naked. He poured Cointreau upon my privates and he set fire to my groin! I was not amused. I said to him, 'Ernie! Lucky Ernie, what the hell is giong on?' And he said to me, 'Soph, when Lucky Ernie goes down, he goes down in flames!'"

At a booksigning for **A View From a Broad,** *Bette wore a hat that looked like a type-writer.*

ELEVEN

Quotable Quotes

"She's really one of those people who come along once every hundred years. There's some odd things about her, being Jewish, raised in Honolulu, some strange and wonderful combination of genetic factors that has produced someone with instincts that are so free, so full, and so deep. She's an American natural resource, and I feel very responsible recording her for history."—Mark Rydell, director, *The Rose* and *For the Boys*

"If Mother Teresa had a child with Sophie Tucker, it would be Bette Midler."—Robin Williams

"Privately, what people don't know about her is that, unlike a lot of funny people, she does not have this need to always be on. She does make me laugh, but it's not out of a need of hers. She's quite introspective and has a tremendous social consciousness. Also, she's one of the most voracious readers I've ever met."—Martin von Haselberg, Bette's husband

"Bette has a terrific voice, but it is more than that. The greatness lies in the spirit; the acting, the passion, and the drive that you think of when you describe a true artist."—Barry Manilow

"Bette is the only artist I know whose appeal is universal. Teeny-boppers, gay guys, gay girls, sixty-five-year-olds, straights. The only audience that she misses is the black audience."—Aaron Russo, personal manager, 1972–79

Alan Bates had a good time working with Bette in **The Rose.**

"I'm blessed to work with her. She really is a fabulous lady and a creative dynamo, and she's a genius. Once you establish that, the rest is easy."—Arif Mardin, record producer, *Beaches, Bette of Roses,* and others

"She's my favorite entertainer."—Tommy Tune, Broadway director-choreographer-performer

"The tenacity of this woman is amazing. She taught me many things—about bravery and taking chances. When I started out with her, I'd never sung backup before for anybody. Going to work with Bette Midler was like going away to show business camp."—Linda Hart, former Harlette

"She's a natural actress. She tries things a hundred different ways, has a tremendous sense of when something's right or wrong, and is quite uncompromising when she's found out."—Alan Bates, costar, *The Rose*

Barbara Hershey found Bette an inspiration when they did Beaches. *(Touchstone)*

"Bette has always been a survivor. She was always trying something new, and she was more cognizant of her assets than anybody else. She always said, 'Let me be the first to do something.' This is a woman with a huge point of view about life."—Melissa Manchester, former Harlette

"What I like about working with Bette is that she wears her whole presence on the outside. If she's mad at you, she comes at you with a knife. If she loves you, she gives you a smile. You never have to worry what she's thinking. It makes it much easier to deal with and gets the work done with great efficiency."—Joe Layton, director, *Clams on the Half-Shell*

"Like most parents, I tended to yell a lot and regret it afterwards. She liked to take charge of things and she was always talking. Our Bette, she was always a yenta."—Fred Midler

"One of the most memorable performances I witnessed while I was ushering took place on New Year's Eve in 1979 when Bette Midler was playing on Broadway. After the conclusion of her three-hour love affair

with a capacity crowd, she asked for the house lights up, band and backup singers silent, and a song from her adoring audience. With the sweetness and innocence of a five-year-old, she said, 'Please sing 'Silent Night' to me.' Then, the Divine Miss M started them off a capella. As their voices grew, she stood silently, listening, drinking in the love that was pouring over her. She cried. We cried. That was theater."—Mary Jo, usherette, in *Playbill*

"She's incredibly gracious and courteous, unbelievably conscientious and hardworking. She really did live up to my expectations, and that's hard because she has a reputation that precedes her."—Sarah Jessica Parker, costar, *Hocus Pocus*

"She's very impetuous, very emotionally responsive, and playing opposite her is a bit like running after a moving train sometimes. She'll throw crazy lines at you and you just have to be ready, and I like that. She's totally unpredictable, and I found that very enjoyable."—Barbara Hershey, co-star, *Beaches*

"If Bette could tap everything she has as an actress, she could play Lady Macbeth."—Paul Mazursky, director, *Down and Out in Beverly Hills* and *Scenes From a Mall*

"I remember one day when we were rehearsing for the film, Bette walked in and she looked like this not-so-attractive girl with a lot on her mind. Then something hit her and she switched on. When that happens, she grows about twelve feet, her breasts are bigger, and her smile warms everything up. Clark Kent runs into a phone booth to become Superman, but Bette runs into a little secret place in her mind and comes out another being."—Peter Coyote, costar, *Outrageous Fortune*

"She spoke in her show about loneliness, about friends. And I remember being so overwhelmed by her: her music, her style, her personality on stage. That mixture of being cantankerous and rude. She made it a lot easier for me coming out. She seemed like someone who really understood the problems of getting free. You know the song 'I Shall Be Released'? When she sang it, I felt that finally, after so many years of despair and not being able to talk about it, well, the song was very important to me."—A Midler fan

"Bette is easy to work with except she demands that everyone work as hard as she does, which is very difficult. It's incredible how much time

she puts in and still performs as a full-time wife and mother. Bette never does anything halfway. Everything is one hundred percent, from throwing a birthday party for Sophie to refining the lyrics for an album. She's a meticulous dynamo. As for her private persona, she's very elegant and at the same time very funny. She has more energy than anyone I know."—Bonnie Bruckheimer, business partner

ON THE OTHER HAND . . .

"Bette Midler is very stupid. She's not a bad person, but stupid in terms of gray matter. I mean, I like her, but I like my dog, too."—James Caan, costar, *For the Boys*

"Attila the Hun would be a relief after Bette. If I had known what I was getting into, I wouldn't have done it."—Ken Wahl, costar, *Jinxed*

"I found it bloody awful. She thinks she is a better director than I am. I've worked with many stars who are difficult, but she's a really tough customer."—Don Siegel, director, *Jinxed*

Don't Touch Me! Ken Wahl hated working with Bette in **Jinxed**.

TWELVE

The Bette Trivia Quiz

1. What role did Bette play on Broadway in *Fiddler on the Roof?*

2. What kind of factory did Bette work in before leaving Hawaii?

3. In *The Rose,* her final hometown concert takes place where?

4. What's the motto for All Girl Productions?

5. True or False: For many years, Bette had a New York City apartment on Greenwich Street.

6. What is Bette's only number one song?

7. What song was Bette's contribution to the children's album *In Harmony: A Sesame Street Record?*

8. Bette has worked in feature films with three different directors twice. Name the directors and the films.

9. Since moving back to New York, what has been Bette's main environmental cleanup charity?

10. Bette's mother named her for Bette Davis. What movie stars were her sisters, Judith and Susan, named after?

11. What was the name of Geraldo Rivera's book that upset Bette so much because he told of their brief sexual encounter?

12. What Midler song became an unofficial inspirational theme for Operation Desert Storm?

The Queen of Compost! What's that New York charity? (Bill Davila/Retna Ltd.)

Sadie ran this company to the max!

13. "Optimistic Voices" on Bette's first album is from what famous musical?

14. What is the name of the company Sadie Shelton runs in *Big Business?*

15. In *Outrageous Fortune*, what was Sandy's lone film credit?

16. In *Stella,* what's the name of the song Stella and Jenny sing together while sewing?

17. In *The First Wives Club* and *Big Business,* Bette is the mother of a little boy, and in both films he has the same name. What is it?

18. One of the following women was never a Harlette: Ula Hedwig, Charlotte Crossley, Melissa Manchester, Maria McKee, Katey Sagal, Linda Hart. Which one?

19. Delores DeLago is the toast of what town?

20. What movie star originated the role of Stella in the first talking version of *Stella Dallas?*

21. From what high school did Bette Midler graduate?

22. In her first engagement in Las Vegas, Bette was the opening act for whom?

23. Although she's practically the same age as Bette, who played her mother in *Beaches?*

24. Who is Clementine?

25. On Bette's first network TV special, which two-time Oscar winner played Rachmaninoff on the piano?

26. Name the artist who drew the images of Bette on her first two album covers.

27. "She gave . . . and gave . . . and gave. Until she had nothing left to give." This is the ad copy for which Bette Midler movie?

28. Who was the choreographer who staged numbers for Bette's concerts before making a hit with the song and video "Hey, Mickey"?

29. In *Clams on the Half-Shell,* what famous musician was part of the revue?

30. When Bette received her special Tony Award, who presented it to her?

31. Bette teamed up with what rock star for the single and video of "Beast of Burden"?

32. One of the following stars did not have Bette as a guest star on his/her TV special: Cher, Neil Diamond, Neil Sedaka, Burt Bacharach, Bing Crosby. Which one?

33. True or False: Bette's first Grammy Award was in the Best New Artist category.

34. Bette once said, "Laurence Olivier changes his nose, I change ———." What was Bette talking about?

35. In what city was *Live at Last* recorded?

36. What Bette Midler movie was the very first Disney picture to get an R rating?

37. Is Bette left- or right-handed?

38. What was the name of the talking cat in *Hocus Pocus*?

39. Bette first met Martin von Haselberg at the Roxy in Los Angeles. Who was performing that night?

40. What five leading men have worked on screen with both Bette Midler and Barbra Streisand?

41. What was the name of the TV show that featured Bette and her husband Martin von Haselberg?

42. What's the name of Barbara and Dave Whiteman's dog in *Down and Out in Beverly Hills*?

43. In which film does Bette yodel?

44. Who is Bette's only leading man who was also once her live-in boyfriend?

45. With whom did Bette sing "Buckets of Rain"?

46. In 1980, Bette won two Golden Globes—for what?

47. What college did Bette attend?

48. Who was the artist who drew the images for *The Saga of Baby Divine*?

49. What was the Cole Porter song Bette did in *Scenes from a Mall*?

50. What song does Bette sing twice on her debut album?

Delores DeLago—a mermaid from what town?

ANSWERS

1. Tzeitel

2. A pineapple factory

3. Miami

4. We Hold a Grudge

5. False. It was on Barrow Street.

6. "Wind Beneath My Wings"

7. "Blueberry Pie"

8. Mark Rydell—*The Rose* and *For the Boys;* Paul Mazursky—*Down and Out in Beverly Hills* and *Scenes From a Mall;* Jim Abrahams—*Ruthless People* and *Big Business*

9. The Manhattan Restoration Project

10. Judy Garland and Susan Hayward

11. *Exposing Myself*

12. "From a Distance"

13. *The Wizard of Oz*

14. Moramax

15. *Ninja Vixens*

16. "California Dreaming"

17. Jason

18. Maria McKee

19. Chicago

20. Barbara Stanwyck

21. Radford High

22. Johnny Carson

23. Lainie Kazan

24. In the Soph and Ernie jokes, she's Sophie's best girlfriend

25. Dustin Hoffman

26. Richard Amsel

27. *The Rose*

28. Toni Basil

29. Lionel Hampton

30. Johnny Carson

31. Mick Jagger

32. Neil Diamond

33. True

34. Her nails

35. Cleveland

36. *Down and Out in Beverly Hills*

37. Right-handed

38. Binx

39. King Crimson

40. George Segal (*For the Boys, The Owl and the Pussycat*), Gene Hackman (*Hawaii, All Night Long*), Nick Nolte (*Down and Out in Beverly Hills, The Prince of Tides*), Richard Dreyfuss (*Down and Out in Beverly Hills, Nuts*) and James Caan (*For the Boys, Funny Lady*)

41. *Mondo Beyondo*

42. Matisse

43. *Big Business*

44. Peter Riegert

45. Bob Dylan

46. Best Actress—Musical/Comedy for *The Rose,* and Best New Artist

47. University of Hawaii

48. Todd Schorr

49. "You Do Something to Me"

50. "Friends"

In the spotlight, Bette comes to life.

THIRTEEN

ou Gotta Have Friends: Bette's Fans

All major stars have their fans . . . and their detractors. The truly biggest stars have even more of both, but the superstars make sure to have more of the former than the latter. In the case of Bette Midler, she has a legion of fans that are truly legendary. Passionate, loyal, large, multi-generational, multi-cultural, and thriving, Bette Midler's fan base is one of the most crucial elements in her success. From the boys who first went to see her at the Continental Baths to the supporters who have never missed her live concerts to the teenage girls who cried their eyes out when she sang "The Glory of Love" in *Beaches* to today's moviegoers who flocked to see *The First Wives Club* over and over again, Bette Midler's fan base shows no signs of waning.

An informal survey of Bette Midler fans conducted for this book via the Internet reveals that Bette's appeal is unique. Her personality as well as her talent attracts admirers. Her sense of humor is key, almost more than her music. Her sustained stardom in movies has won her millions of new fans and kept her older fans connected to her.

If you were to create a blueprint for success, Midler's career would be a viable model. From live appearances to records to television to movies to books—and then back again—Bette has given audiences numerous chances to sample her wares and become hooked for life. In many ways, once a Midler fan always a Midler fan. The fans stick with Bette through all the various media she conquers. There is a sense that they know her. As one person explained it, "She is real, people can relate to her. Her head isn't in the clouds, she's down to earth. She cares, she loves, she sings, she dances, she tells jokes, she acts, she is incredible. Bette Midler decided she was going to be somebody, and look at her now. There is no bullshit about the Divine Miss M! What makes Bette Midler so special, she's made of some really awesome stuff." Another fan concurred: "She has grown into an entertainer without compare. She does it all and gives her all, touching your heart and lifting your soul." Another had a similar take: "She gives her audiences the thrill of their lives and she loves doing it. She has the ability to play off of her audience. She's also a fabulous person."

As the new century approaches, there is little doubt that Bette Midler, one of the twentieth century's very best, will continue to be one of the world's most beloved stars.

The fan survey encompassed many aspects of Bette's appeal, beginning with a question about how one became a Bette Midler fan in the first place. The number one response was from her films, followed by her music or concert work. Thanks primarily to the very prolific Disney years—most of the eighties—Bette Midler won a completely new generation of fans. The film work was constant and widely distributed, and it continues to win her new fans in video and television airings. And when she scores a major hit like *The First Wives Club,* more and more people are exposed to her talent and become fans. It's a self-perpetuating process.

Question two of the survey asked fans to identify their favorite Midler moment, what they hold as a cherished memory. By and large, seeing Bette live in concert was the top response. Thanks to her many years of concert touring—in particular, the *Experience The Divine* show, which played dozens of cities in 1993 and 1994—fans have had the opporunity to see the Divine Miss M on stage. Compared to someone like Barbra Streisand, who didn't tour for twenty-eight years before doing twenty-six concerts in 1994, Bette has been far more accessible. In fact, many Midler fans have seen Bette live in concert more than once, comparing personal memories from *Clams on the Half-Shell* to *De Tour* to *Experience the Divine.* Even though ten years passed between *De Tour* and *Experience the Divine,* fans hold the memories of her shows in high regard and do not feel at all distant from the diva. As the following respondent's story reveals, Bette has had a great ability to touch her audiences—figuratively and literally: "My favorite [memory] is when she was in concert in St. Louis. It was my first Bette concert and I had second-row seats. I bought a rose from one of those girls that sell them at the concert. She was singing 'Wind Beneath My Wings' and I decided to take the rose up to her. There were lots of people around me, but the Divine one decided to take my rose, hold my hand, and sing a whole verse of the song looking right at me."

When asked to explain what makes Bette Midler special, a variety of responses were offered. Interestingly enough, the top reason was Bette's stature as a person, an artist, a woman, and a humanitarian. Many consider her a leader: "She is a true inspiration to many people. I hope she realizes what a national treasure she really is." To others, she is more than that: "Bette's a person many people look up to as a role model, even me. Most people want to be like her." Another fan detailed the profound effect Bette has had on her life, explaining, "It sounds corny to say that Bette Midler changed my life, but I really believe that she did. After finding out about her, her life, her career, her philosophy, I found the courage within myself to go back to school, to get another job, and, most importantly, to learn to love myself for who I am, not who others think I should be. I learned to 'cherish forever what makes [me] unique.' I think everyone, at one time or another in his/her life, feels like an outcast. But Bette urges us to celebrate our differences. . . . I can say without any reservations whatsoever that I am a better person because of Bette Midler."

Second to her personality and strength, fans revere Bette's talent. One respondent wrote, "Her voice is that of an angel. Her movies are the absolute best. She puts her all into everything she does. She seems so very down to earth, but not too much that would make her normal. She is just the best!" Another also compared her vocal talent to Heaven. "She has the most wholesome, beautiful voice that I've ever heard. The only thing I can compare her voice to is that of an angel. Bette has a certain aura to her entire being. Her smile can light up a room."

Midler fans also sense in Bette qualities that they would like in a friend: honesty, trustworthiness, and innate goodness. "Bette Midler has a heart and soul of gold. Her true personality echoes through her laughter and song," wrote one. Another said, "She's real down to earth, one of the last few performers to have real talent." One more respondent explained, "Bette is the most entertaining person in the business. She is certainly my ideal mom. A great singer, actress, and homebody. I watch her videos over and over. My kids know most of her Sophie Tucker jokes by heart. I quote her often." Another fan put it like this: "She knew what she wanted and she went out and got it. And also, I think that she is extremely talented, and I would like more than anything to be like her." Finally, one respondent concluded, "I like her humor and her compassion. Her humanity and compassion seep through everything, even the risqué routines. I believe that is why everyone loves her so much. . . . because she's human."

When describing what makes Midler so unique, many fans talked of how she has changed them personally: "After my grandmother's death, Bette's music kept me alive. . . . I felt isolated, but I had Bette's music. . . . Even though my life is only twenty years long, the road has been hard and Bette has been there for every high and every low . . . even though she doesn't know I exist. I thank God for her. I honestly believe she has helped me get through life without giving up. Bette Midler holds a special place in my heart and I can only hope to thank her someday."

One respondent recalled the exact moment he became a Midler fan. "On the night that Johnny Carson special was on, I just happened to be watching TV and there she was . . . this short, at that time very pudgy, little woman with bright red hair. I watched transfixed as this little force of nature pranced around in front of Mr. Carson's desk, leapt up on top of it, shook her cleavage in his face, and, for the finale, kicked her tiny stiletto heels off her feet and into the air. All this while singing an utterly hilarious, self-deprecating tune called 'Fat as I Am.' I never knew Bette Midler could be like this! All I'd seen of her in the past was wild hairdos, wild clothes, and wild, unabashedly risqué jokes. For years, I'd heard people carry on about how talented she was, but, to be completely honest, I'd never thought so. Then again, to borrow a quote from her last tour, I'd 'never really experienced the Divine.'"

The survey asked respondents to name their three favorite Bette Midler films, and the top three responses were *Beaches, The Rose,* and *For the Boys. Beaches* was number one by a large margin. With its blend of humor, music, emotional conflict, and enduring friendship, it is in many ways the quintessential Bette Midler experience. And in C.C. Bloom, Bette had a character who was perhaps as close to her true self as any will ever be. These elements combine to make *Beaches* a unique project in Bette Midler's filmography, and it will always have a special place in the hearts of fans. One said, "The entire *Beaches* experience was something that changed my life. During this, the roughest time of my life, I found Bette Midler. This sounds so silly now, but I remember that during that time the only thing I looked forward to was my trip to and from school in the morning and afternoon listening to the *Beaches* album." Considering the success of *The Rose,* it is not too surprising that it also ranks so high with fans. It is not only Bette's first film, but it is also an Academy Award–nominated performance. Bette Midler might be pleasantly surprised to learn that her fans regard *For the Boys* so highly, especially since she was so disappointed with its pedestrian box office success. Interestingly, even though *The First Wives Club* was Bette's most recent picture when the survey was done—and a huge blockbuster at that—it ranked number five among our fan respondents.

Another question concerned the characters Midler has created—in film and on stage. When asked to assess the most memorable of all, the Rose (from the film of the same name) was the leader, followed by Delores DeLago, Bette's concertizing mermaid in a wheelchair. Tied for third place were C.C. Bloom (*Beaches*) and Mama Rose (*Gypsy*). The Rose, considered by most as Bette's saddest character and her finest acting achievement, impressed one respondent in this way: "[She is] the most memorable Bette character. She was riveting. I don't cry at many movies, but that was the first movie I ever shed a tear over. It was a magnificent performance." Her lounge lizard songstress, Delores DeLago, is equally well loved. Soph, the ribald, bawdy teller of dirty jokes modeled after Sophie Tucker, is another fan favorite, followed by the two Sadies in *Big Business.*

The survey inquired about favorite Bette Midler songs. The top three read like Bette's greatest hits: "The Rose," "The Wind Beneath My Wings," and "From a Distance." They ranked in just that order. After these "inspirational ballads," as Bette likes to call them, fans are much more eclectic in their choice. The list of favorites includes "Miss Otis Regrets," "Stay With Me," "To Deserve You," "Twisted," "Storybook Children," "To Comfort You," "Otto Titsling," and "I Believe in You," all of which received multiple mentions. Other songs cited were "Do You Want to Dance?," "Stuff Like That There," "Oh, Industry," "Shiver Me Timber," "God Help the Outcasts," "Friends," "Heart Over Head," "I Know You By Heart," "It's Gonna Rain," "Rain," "Married Men," "Millworker," "You Don't Own Me," "It Is Love," "My Mother's Eyes," "Moonlight Dancing," and "One for the Road." What is missing from this list is the very first song that brought Bette any notoriety at all, "Boogie Woogie Bugle Boy," a song Midler has always included in every live concert performance. Another omission is "I Shall Be Released," a long-revered Midler cover that has brought her great acclaim.

The inclusion of "Do You Want to Dance?" spurred one respondent to recall how hearing that song reached him, and why he still loves it so: "It was the summer of '73 and I was seventeen years old. I was lonely, depressed, and coming to terms with my homosexuality. I heard Bette sing 'Do You Want to Dance?' over the radio and was immediately drawn to that powerful, moving, and emotion-filled voice. I had no idea she was fast becoming a gay icon, I just knew she touched me in a way no other singer had before."

The survey asked respondents to name their three favorite albums—the three they would take with them to a desert island! *Bette of Roses, Experience the Divine,* and *Live at Last* were the three most often cited by fans. In these selections, logic ruled: *Bette of Roses* is Midler's most recent album, therefore it has top-of-mind recognition; *Experience the Divine* is her first and only greatest hits collection, therefore it covers all the bases; and *Live at Last* has the best of Bette, her jokes, her spontaneity, and her music. *Beaches* was the next most popular album. *Some People's Lives* and *Songs for the New Depression* followed, even though the latter album was never a big hit, much to Bette's chagrin. Clearly, it reached the die-hard fans and they still love it. *Thighs and Whispers, Broken Blossom, No Frills, Divine Madness, The Rose,* and *Bette Midler* each had a few mentions, as did the soundtracks for *The First Wives Club, Gypsy* and *For the Boys.* The most shocking omission in this group of albums is *The Divine Miss M,* Bette's debut album. Despite containing many of the songs that are Bette Midler standards, including "Friends," "Do You Want to Dance," and "Boogie Woogie Bugle Boy," it failed to get even a single mention from the respondents.

When asked to name any other stars they rate as highly as Bette Midler, this group of fans—by a margin of two to one—claimed that nobody else rates that high. The only other two who received more than one vote were Barbra Streisand and Rosie O'Donnell. The other celebrities garnering mentions were Audrey Hepburn, Oprah Winfrey, Loretta Lynn, Carolyn Jones, Shirley MacLaine, Julie Andrews, Whoopi Goldberg, and Janet Jackson.

Finally, respondents were asked what they would like to say to Bette Midler if they ever had the chance to meet her face to face. The overriding sentiment among fans is that they would like to thank her. "I just would like to thank her for everything and ask her to keep up the good work—her work makes many people smile every single day! She is one of a kind, and when she goes, so will the greatest thing about show business! She has been a friend to me, and many others, and I am sure that she will never know this, or 'get' it, or maybe even care. If she ever needed a kidney, I'd donate." Another respondent reiterated that feeling: "I would thank her from the bottom of my heart for all that she has given me through her music, films, and concerts. I would thank her for being the great humanitarian she is and how it has made me a more responsible person by recycling and giving generously to AIDS research."

Respondents also said that they would want to talk to Bette about life and tell her why they care, how she changed their lives, and why they feel she's so great. "She makes those of us who have been cursed as 'do-gooders' feel as if we are being mischievous for

With Martin von Haselberg before the annual American Museum of the Moving Image Tribute Dinner (UPI/Corbis-Bettman)

just a few hours. She is a 'do-gooder' and she gets up there and says or does a few bawdy things. The fans just feel like 'Yeah, Bette, let your hair down.' Her energy is something for each of us to strive for, as is her persistence, and her wonderful outlook on life. She helped me, as an awkward teenager, to feel as if I really could do anything I set out to do—and I now believe that." Still another explained, "I can't imagine my life without her. I began my affair with her at seventeen, I look forward to all Bette has yet to give and share with her fans."

In conclusion, to her fans, Bette Midler is more than entertainment, more than merely a celebrity, and more than just someone who has survived. As one respondent said, "Throughout her career she has said and done so many outrageous things. She has led the way for many to follow. She is also very honest and very forthright. This combination makes for a wild package that can only be Bette Midler."

For the Boys **was an important film in Bette's career.**

Acknowledgments

There are many people who have helped in the creation of this scrap-book; first and foremost, my husband Leslie Solow, who has been a supportive, understanding, and creative partner since day one. To my parents—Jean and Hy—a heartfelt thanks for always loving me and especially for being my foundation through the past year and all the trials I have had to endure. To Shelley, Elliot, Mitch, Nancy, Ellen, Mark, Meryll, Sam . . . thanks for everything.

To the friends I have met through Bette, thank you all for your generosity, your encouragement, and your unfailing spirit. You reflect the best of Bette! Thanks, Michael Gillespie, Carl V. Sampson, Mandy Clark, Jill Prince, Jess Kimball, and the many Bette fans on America Online and Prodigy bulletin boards.

In particular, I wish to express gratitude to Paul Katz and Bob Massre, who opened their arms and shared their collections; to Rafe Chase, Todd Sussman, and Guy Vespoint, who provided excellent sounding boards; to James Spada, Chris Nickens, and Karen Swenson, for laying the groundwork; to Sue Cragg, Linda Goldstone, Steve Baxter, Tom Gilbert, and Rich Bozanich, who were always on the lookout for me; to Jerry Ohlinger for sharing material; to Walter McBride at Retna Ltd. for his able assistance and keen eye; to Mary Keesling, who dug deep and helped me in a hundred different ways, but especially for being my dearest friend.

Once upon a time, Bette sang about "Friends." To everyone who has comprised Bette's loyal and large fandom—all those friends—thanks to you, too. This book is truly for you.

Finally, I wish to acknowledge Bette Midler for making the

world take notice. With her music, her films, her sense of humor, and her indomitable spirit, she has made this world a much brighter place. This scrapbook is a reflection of one very divine life.

—Allison J. Waldman

Photo Credits

Unless otherwise noted, all the photos and poster reproductions in this book are courtesy of the film producing companies—20th Century Fox, United Artists, Disney, and Paramount Pictures. Additionally, the author gratefully acknowledges photographs provided by Atlantic Records, NBC Television, and HBO.